WILD WOMAN

WILD WOMAN

Empowering Stories from Women who Work in Nature

Philippa Forrester

BLOOMSBURY WILDLIFE
LONDON • OXFORD • NEW YORK • NEW DELHI • SYDNEY

BLOOMSBURY WILDLIFE
Bloomsbury Publishing Plc
50 Bedford Square, London, WC1B 3DP, UK
29 Earlsfort Terrace, Dublin 2, Ireland

BLOOMSBURY, BLOOMSBURY WILDLIFE and the Diana logo are trademarks of
Bloomsbury Publishing Plc

First published in the United Kingdom in 2024

A catalogue record for this book is available from the British Library

Library of Congress Cataloguing-in-Publication data has been applied for

ISBN: HB: 978-1-3994-0087-9; ePub: 978-1-3994-0085-5; ePDF: 978-1-3994-0090-9;
audio: 978-1-3994-0088-6

4 6 8 10 9 7 5 3

Typeset in Bembo Std by Deanta Global Publishing Services, Chennai, India
Printed and bound in Great Britain by CPI Group (UK) Ltd, Croydon CR0 4YY

To find out more about our authors and books visit www.bloomsbury.com
and sign up for our newsletters

Contents

Look deep into nature, and then you will understand everything better.

Albert Einstein

A Tsunami of the Soul

Was I wild? Too right. Life had taken a rather ugly turn. So what was I going to do about it?

Many people return from the wilderness triumphant. Not I. My return to the UK from the wilds of Wyoming and our big family adventure was utterly dismal. I was even more so. There was no more big family adventure. There was no more big family. Only pain and confusion.

The End.

Well, it felt like that to me.

———

At my feet, I saw a grizzly print — so fresh that the mud was still oozing, terror crept into my bones and sank my stomach. The memory of it still gave me the shivers — yet that was nothing compared to the mind-numbing reality I now faced, in fact now I longed for that.

Distraught at the end of my marriage. Missing my husband and best friend terribly. My family fragmented and so many of the dear, loving relationships around us suddenly strange and strained. I found myself feeling alone and frightened. Feeling somewhat self-indulgent and ungrateful, I would very much have appreciated a grizzly bear incident to have finished me off nicely — anything seemed better than accepting what life was throwing at me — but no such luck in the UK. In fact, here, I could go outside covered in honey and scream my head off, and not one bear would come and eat me.

Fight or flight was really kicking in. In truth, it had been a constant state for so long that I knew I had finally run out of fight. I had used every tool in my toolbox's lifelong collection to remain a person of integrity, purpose and

happiness, but those tools just weren't working now and the
punches kept coming.

All my life, when the proverbial is hitting the fan or when
I'm just feeling the blues, a good dollop of gratitude hits the
spot for me like the warmth of a decent malt hitting the
gullet, spreading good vibes and smiles all around. Not now.
The gratitude journal might as well gather cobwebs for all
the use it was. Cognitively, I knew I had so much to be
grateful for: three amazing sons, a beautiful roof over our
healthy heads, many friends and their utter determination to
get me back to *me*. I am so grateful for . . . I could say it, I
just couldn't feel it. I was numb.

If gratitude wasn't hitting the spot, then how about
meditation? Nope. At the bit where I was meant to let the
thoughts pass over me like clouds, they simply gathered up
into a tornado and sucked me up. I came out of a meditation
session feeling more like a screaming banshee than buddha.

Journalling, if I'm honest, was nothing more than ranting.
As for writing anything remotely creative – forget that, my
scrambled brain was suddenly no longer capable.

Yoga had always made me feel good, up to then anyway. I
signed up for online classes as we were in lockdown. I knew
they needed to be power ones, the only ones that would
grab my whole attention, but somehow yoga simply
activated my tear ducts. Perhaps it was the 'release'. Anyway,
I was the thumbnail in the corner of the screen doing my
downward dog backward, reluctant to show my face because
I had tears streaming down my forehead and the dog was
licking them off.

Exercise had always been my constant love, another go-to,
another important part of simply being me. Now, the only
position that was remotely comfortable was foetal. I simply
couldn't. Something inside was broken.

The stakes were higher than ever: three boys and a dog
were relying on me to get my shit together, earn some money,
support them through their own emotional turmoil and be

an amazing mum. Yet sometimes I had to concentrate on simply one left and one right step to keep the panic at bay.

Not even giving myself a good talking-to worked. My British stiff upper lip gave way to a wobbly lower one every time and any morale-boosting talk turned into a string of garbage insults about how utterly useless I was – fat, boring, ugly, shallow and now too emotional . . . All the reasons, all the voices coming back to haunt me. I was beginning to believe those voices, that there must indeed be something very wrong with me. So, back to handing myself over to the grizzly and back to missing the wilderness and— *Seriously? You're crying about the fact that there are no bears outside the front door now? Get a grip, woman.*

I came to the conclusion – unwillingly dragged there by my hair – that I had run out of tools. That the depression, which had started its sneaky infestation with menopause, family deaths, cancer in my son's beautiful brain and finally my husband's change of heart, was finally winning. At the very moment I came home, to a lonely land of Covid isolation, depression was twisting its knife, playing its winning hand. Everything became too much. I simply couldn't fight it.

So, flight? Well, it is always an option but my husband had taken that one, and the three amazing boys and the one particularly wonderful dog still held me in their loving grips. I wasn't going to flee, I knew that. I did hide under the duvet for days at a time and, when I tentatively peered back out, the fact remained that, despite all the things I had to be grateful for, there was no joy. The grief over leaving my wild home in America and all my friends – on top of the relentless pain of losing my husband, the man I loved and thought loved me – became too much.

It also turns out that 'under the duvet' doesn't really work the same as 'in an African beach hut': it doesn't last very long because someone inevitably comes in and asks what they can have to eat, or the dog's earnest Paddington stare lets me know he desperately needs a walk. And so I went through the motions. I got our finances straight, I started a business, I wrote and wrote and wrote, filling journals with utter nonsense. I cooked and sorted and built beds, laid patios, fixed plumbing and electrics and recreated and repaired our home.

And the fact remained: there was no joy.

AUTUMN

CHAPTER ONE

The True Power of a Machete

The clocks have changed. Ah, the perpetuity of time and nature.

'Is this winter? This isn't winter,' says my youngest as we bump down the lane, avoiding the potholes that the council always seem to be fixing but never actually fix.

'It's winter in the UK.'

'But where's the snow? This is, like, just wet and cold.'

'Exactly.'

We cross the bridge that leads to our home, over the mud-laden roaring river in water-laden gloam and gloom. Bags are slung, shoes abandoned and it's time to get the dinner on.

Never mind the outside, I can't ignore the damp and the cold seeping into the house either. We are overdue a heating oil delivery. I have finally got enough in the bank account and organised more oil; the heating should have kicked in by now, so why was it cold? When I call the supplier, it turns out that there was no oil in the tank after all – our complicated delivery system has failed us.

'They came to deliver today but they couldn't get there.'

'I see.'

'It's too overgrown and now there are some fallen trees too.'

'Right.'

I'm tired, beyond tired.

'We really need to get it filled before the heating tries to draw any more oil down; otherwise you'll have a repair bill on your hands when all the bits at the bottom of the tank start clogging up your pipes,' says Andy, our lovely oil man. 'I can't get there tomorrow but I can put you in for Monday. It's a big job, do you think you can have it done for then?'

'Don't worry, we'll have it all done for Monday,' I manage breezily.

This stuff was always my husband's department. Now it's mine.

When we turned two old mill workers' cottages into one house, one thing we were keen to change was the oil delivery system. We really wanted no oil at all but to have a ground-source heat pump instead because, even decades ago, I was ecologically minded and I knew it would be way more environmentally friendly. Yet the builders had declared themselves bankrupt by that stage and nearly taken us down with them, so it was taking every penny we had just to get a roof on and windows in.

When money is tight, environmental concerns seem to become a luxury. Despite that, we did still manage to change some things. The old mill cottages had oil-fired central heating and hot water but the oil had to be delivered via a pipe over the river and we did not like that one bit. This was the same river that otters had returned to, that kingfishers dived into, and where every year, trout and mayfly would rise together, and ducklings take their first swim. And yet, the tanker would park in the driveway and the pipe would be dragged across the flood meadow and over the bridge to the oil tank, which was just feet from the riverbank and precariously balanced on bricks. All in all, it was too risky. One spill could pollute the river horrifically. The more we knew about the wildlife on the river, the more protective we were of it. That way wasn't going to be acceptable. So, we came up with another solution that wasn't ideal but didn't compromise the river.

The oil would be delivered to a tank at the back of the garden, as far away from the river as we could get it but also, rather inconveniently, as far away from the road as it could be. So, in the absence of four-wheel-drive, off-road oil lorries, we had to dig a very long trench. It went all the way from the new, safe oil tank, across a field to the lane. In it we laid a pipe so that we could fill up from the roadside and the oil didn't go near the river at any point in the process.

Fast-forward to now. When I last saw the field, prior to moving to Wyoming and renting out our house, it was a neatly mown meadow with some wildlife ponds and trees, but that was many years ago. Nature has since had her own way and the following morning, I see for myself that the results of her work are pretty astounding.

The back gate leading to the oil tank and field is rotten, so just one push and it falls off its hinges and collapses. All that remains of any integrity is the bright shiny door catch dangling off the post and glinting in the sunshine. I step through the gap and into the meadow. I'm met with rather a shock; the whole place is bramble, twice the height of me. I can barely even see a way through. I sidle around the edge, plucking the grasping bramble branches from my clothes and hair, and manage to make it all the way to the lane. I wonder if any remaining path might look clearer from here but only find it is worse and now I can clearly see why the oil delivery guys simply couldn't get in. The way from the road to the filling nozzle is not only shrouded in brambles but trees have fallen at angles across it, blocking it completely unless you were to clamber up, squeeze between them, get your hair caught in thorns and rip up your jeans. Which is, of course, what I do. The bramble molestation continues until I finally get to the tank and peer inside. I can just about see a shallow puddle at the bottom, but there really is nothing left.

I return to the house to galvanise the teenage army of one.

'Let's do this,' I say to Fred, who, having just motivated himself out of his bedroom, has a different agenda. His first thought is FaceTiming his girlfriend, who is just waking up in the US. It is also his second and third thought, rapidly followed by: 'What can I have to eat?' I would have to be an imbecile not to notice there isn't really much enthusiasm for chainsawing and clearing brambles, and a ridiculous optimist at thinking I could inspire him.

Finally, because he has a good heart, he does concede enough to walk around the lane with me to take a look. After a deep sigh, he tells me he will get on to it later when his 'work clothes' are out of the wash. That is at least good news; up until now I had no idea such clothes existed in his wardrobe.

Between work, cooking and shopping for groceries, the afternoon escapes quickly, compounded by the light failing unexpectedly early because the clocks have changed. So, with little choice, I stomp back up to the paddock with a chainsaw and machete.

'I've got this,' I mutter grumpily. Then, more British as I regard the scene, 'Bloody positive Americanisms.' At this point I should have known there would be a wobbly chin ahead.

The chainsaw is, as ever, reluctant to start work too. It's always been a bit moody. However, today I have no patience for its vagaries so I'm determined to show it who is boss. After nearly dislocating my shoulder with the pull cord as I try to get it started, I begin cutting through the trunk of the first half-fallen blackthorn tree which lies at a ridiculous angle blocking the way, but I'm not even halfway when it creaks and groans and then abruptly rips apart. Part of it falls, dragging another tree with it, ensuring that both now add to the blocked-path conundrum. Not only that, but their top branches now splay out across the road in the path of any oncoming traffic.

I probably didn't plan this very well. Classic. Maybe I should have had a better method. Perhaps I should have started with the small bits at the ends first to take the weight off the trunk and then work my way down. Well, there isn't time to tango with hindsight now. I need to work faster, before someone comes speeding down the lane in an inappropriate vehicle (anything but a tractor would do it), crashes into my fallen trees and decides to sue me for the one $50 note I have left. Besides, time is cracking on and I have to pick the kids up from school.

So, now that the branches are in the road, I do start with the smaller bits. I don't have time to process them properly, though, so, in a slightly furious fashion, I cut them all into the biggest pieces I can and manhandle them onto the bank.

Blackthorn may look pretty in the spring with its clouds of small white flowers bursting forth, or in the autumn when its purple sloes shine, beckoning thoughts of cosy winters and sloe gin, and it may well provide a safe nesting place for birds and a sheltered corridor for small mammals to move about the countryside, but let me tell you, it also has vicious thorns at least an inch long. They stab at my face, hair and arms and they hurt a lot and I remember that often the wound from a blackthorn can get swollen and painful long after the encounter because they are somehow dangerous. I find I am not in the best of moods – actually I'm swearing my head off.

I glance up as I hear people approaching. Another sight new to me since my return: a group of lycra-wrapped lockdown lovelies power-walking by, ponytails up high, buttocks up higher, clad in slick, clean leggings and with matching water bottles in hand. To my knowledge, no one ever 'power-walked' up and down the lane when we lived here before. As they walk by they stop their cheery gossiping, stare at me and the mess, smile politely, pick their way across the branches and then a little further down the lane they actually start giggling.

That, right there, threatens to launch me into full-on victim mode. I had been fighting it off, teetering on the brink of feeling sorry for myself, being a capable woman with a chainsaw, but that is not going to happen now. *Stop it.* I remind myself that there are far worse places to be, *you live in a beautiful home and you are lucky to be able to heat it, you have an amazing place with trees and wildlife. You've got this.* 'Now,' I tell myself out loud in a businesslike and uplifting manner, 'just chop the massive branch into small logs and then the first tree is done and the bonus is that we have more firewood.'

But my brain isn't listening. Instead, it's flashing back to Daphne, our old neighbour – grief-stricken at having lost her husband of many years – proudly telling me that she had 'hedged' this bit of the field all by herself because it was getting overgrown and falling into the lane. Nearly twenty years later, I am alone, grief-stricken, doing the exact same job.

Now I am really teetering, my eyes watering as I stare into the black hole of victimhood. *Nope, not going there.* Another neat log, another neat log. Then with a slur the chainsaw gives up.

'You're giving up on me now?' I ask it. 'Right now? When we are in the thick of it, in the middle of the hard bit?'

It doesn't reply. And now I can't finish the job, and branches are everywhere and I should be working at my desk anyway, and it's going to get dark soon and my hands are bleeding because I forgot my gloves, and the school day is nearly over, and the kids are finding it hard to settle, and I miss the wilderness of Jackson where I didn't have to worry about managing paths, and I hate doing this on my own, and and and . . .

I clearly can't cry in the lane in case the lockdown lovelies come back, so I climb over the gate and into the field.

I remember what it used to look like before we left, all grass and ponds for our rescue otters. Now I stare at the wall of brambles and suddenly I just want to go back there. I want to go back in time so badly to when my boys were tiny and happy, my husband was sitting on a mini digger with a big grin on his face, him and my beloved father-in-law building a pond for an otter. I want to go back to when I had never been happier. I don't want any of the last few years to have happened, I just want to go back.

I grab the machete and walk into the field. The otter ponds must still be here somewhere. Through the dense blackthorn and right into the brambles, away from the lane, away from all of it, heading back in time, I just start hacking.

I've never been good with a machete. We have loads of them in the house, collected from various trips to the Amazon but, try as I might, even after having watched them in use in the jungle, I can never get it right; it still feels like I'm using a butter knife to slice my way through undergrowth.

I really couldn't care, I just want to lose myself and whack stuff. The brambles snatch at my hair again but now, impatient, I pull roughly away. At that moment nature decides to stick a thorn right into my eye, so hard that at first I think my eyeball might have popped. It stings like hell. But I close it and keep going, a bramble branch grazing my cheek and others grabbing at my jeans. I can't see through them or over them. Quickly I'm lost in this mini wilderness. I want to be.

So here it is, nature has got the best of me, and primitive victim mode has taken over. I think about the recent endings I've experienced and what I don't want. I think about my husband starting again with someone new, and . . . *slash!* Suddenly a miracle happens: the force. It takes me so much by surprise that all my raging ceases immediately and I stand still. It is like a laser-focused energy coming from me through the machete and slicing clean through a large branch – this must be what it's like to use a light sabre! *Feel the force, Luke.*

'Was that it?'

I'm talking to myself, properly bananas.

'Let's try this again.'

I think about another painful moment, close my eyes and . . . *slash!* And there it is, laser-sharp and slicing with ease straight through the brambles, just like I have seen in the Amazon, but I actually feel this physically, the focus of energy, the power of the pain. The third . . . and the fourth

. . . and there . . . and there . . . and I'm moving, I'm stepping
slowly through the jungle, creating a path through what
seems like an impenetrable wall, slicing, feeling my machete
as a light sabre. Until, all of a sudden, I reach the fence built
to protect our young, orphaned otters from foxes, people
and badgers. He did a good job, my husband; it still stands
tall, impermeable, the enclosure inside clear of brambles. I
see a glint of water, the pond is still there, and a few extra
saplings have nurtured themselves into existence.

So here we are, face to face, the memories and me. The
enclosure reminds me that it was all real, that I didn't make
our happiness up. And now that the brambles surround me,
protect me, hide me, I cling on to the fence and I weep. I
weep because I miss him so badly, because I can't bear to
raise our teenagers alone, because I can't bear to leave these
memories behind, because it feels like life will never be that
good again, because everyone tells me I should be over that
asshole by now but I miss him so damn much. Because I
won't believe that our marriage was a disaster, and I cry for
a time when I still believed in love. I cry and cry until my
thorn-dented eye stings so much that I can't open it at all.

I wonder if I can climb in and inspect the pond, but I
remember there is a high-wire overhang to stop otters
escaping and so I might not get back out and no one knows
where I am. The gate is way over on the other side of the
large enclosure, brambles take up every inch and – despite
my new technique – it would take hours to get round there,
and it's going to get dark soon.

I'm done. My visit with the past is over. Like Prince
Charming, I hacked my way through the jungle and found
my Sleeping Beauty – I just didn't get a snog out of it. My
intimate and rather unpredicted moment with the wilderness
is done for the day. I head home, change and do a housewifely
chore – stick chilli in the oven.

On the way back from the school run, I decide to stop on
the lane to show my sons exactly what we will need to do

before the weekend is over. They moan, of course, and I don't blame them; it was me who decided a rural life would be good for us all. Perhaps I should have stayed in a city where they could have a 'normal life'. Perhaps trying to make it work here was a mistake; it was me who felt the pull of a life surrounded by the natural world. I made that decision – perhaps it was the wrong one.

When we pull up, there is nothing to see, no work for me to point out. The whole area is already clear. While I have been battling with traffic on the school run, Fred has done it – my teenage hero-in-disguise and in clean 'work clothes'. Hope. And, whether I wanted it to or not, I realise that my little wilderness has just wrestled me through some grieving and shown me some strength I didn't think I had.

I didn't believe I could find any challenging wilderness here in the UK, so it's got me curious. Was I wild? You bet I was, but what did that actually mean? Nature had just given me a slap round the face and told me to pull myself together. Virginia Woolf spoke of a room of her own. I have my own slice of wild, an enormous privilege, what has happened in my absence proves again to me that I am merely its caretaker for a time, that I am witness to and helper of nature here.

Could this little piece of wilderness that I was lucky enough to look after actually be a gift that could lead me back to my resilience and strength, my inspiration and my joy, and help me get through this pain?

CHAPTER TWO

What Really is a Wild Woman, then?

When I started to think about it, about what the natural world could mean, not just for me but for other women, and then what women could mean for the natural world, I found I had even more questions. You know how it is when thoughts like that start to creep in? Suddenly you are noticing those things everywhere, even in the most dreary jobs, like unpacking boxes.

We really did have a lot of books; I find it unbearable to part with them. As I unload the many boxes which haven't seen the light of day since we moved to the US, I realise I am rediscovering my life story told in books, but I'm now also seeing the picture of a woman who has always been interested in the wild world and the animals who inhabit it. The complete works of James Herriot, a series I knew practically off by heart as a child. All the works of Gerald Durrell, the alcoholic zookeeper who broke ground in conservation work. Other much-loved stories too. So many conservation and ecology books, by so many men. Where are the women here? Then Joseph Campbell and Carl Jung, essential reading during my English literature degree.

As is the way with unpacking, I can't simply put them on the shelf. I have to have a quick flick through. I find myself smiling as I read. I remember this stuff. I remember the me who used to read this stuff before I started folding people's underpants for a living.

Joseph Campbell identified arguably the most popular story structure humans have, 'the hero's journey'. Humans across space and time – in all parts of the world, whatever their culture or religion – have been inexplicably drawn to this story structure and replicated it in their own ways,

Star Wars being the most obvious example. There is the 'call
to adventure', like when Luke returns to find his house
burned down and his parents gone. Campbell coined the
idea that every story has a hero – 'Or a heroine,' I mutter.
After the call to adventure, a little shaken, our heroine begins
down the 'road of trials'. This is a bit of a nightmare, to be
honest. There might be goblins and trolls to deal with if you
are a hobbit, or Stormtroopers lurking around the corner, or
there could be brambles. Whatever they are, you have to deal
with each and every obstacle if you are going to make it
down the road of trials. And if you are a woman there are
other pressures, like making sure your mascara doesn't run
or remembering to wear your sports bra while you are
shooting an arrow at an orc from the back of a galloping
horse. Perhaps that is why there aren't many women in this
landscape. Anyway, once you have hit the road of trials there
is no going back . . . I move on.

It's a little like revising. Remembering, from my book
collection, who I was. Not the wavy perm or the aerobics
addiction perhaps, but something more consistent.

'Marriage,' I read in my Joseph Campbell notes, 'and
death ceremonies have a lot in common.' I decide to leave
that bit for now.

After a little more page-flipping, it turns out that
Campbell has a lot, for a man, to say about women or, to put
it more precisely, about female archetypes. I wasn't as
interested in this part of his work when I was learning it the
first time around though.

'The woman does give birth as the earth gives birth to
the plants. She gives nourishment as the plants do. So woman
magic and earth magic are the same, they are related and the
personification then of this energy which gives birth to
forms and nourishes forms is properly female. And so it is in
the agricultural world of ancient Mesopotamia, the Egyptian
Nile but also in the earlier planting systems that the goddess
is the earlier mythic form that is dominant.'[1]

'When you have the goddess as the creator it is her own body that is the universe. When you move to a philosophical point of view the female represents time and space itself, she is time and space and the mystery beyond her is beyond opposites, beyond male and female . . . the gods are her children . . . Everything you can think of, everything you can see is the production of the goddess.'[2]

Crikey, who knew? Perhaps I'm taking more notice because I'm a mother now. Does that make me a goddess then? The author of *The Contented Little Baby Book* (a book I can definitely get rid of) never mentioned that. Mind you, she didn't mention the need to nip to the shops or have a glass of wine with your mates in her self-sacrificial timetable either.

Once he got together with Jung, there was no stopping Campbell. They both identified the idea that myths and stories are the dreams of cultures, that they hold similarities and keys to our human experience and the way we try to comprehend it. But then Jung added in the idea of the collective unconscious. This was the idea that we weren't all just playing a random guessing game and happening to come up with the same stories and dreams, but that there was something deeper going on with humanity, something we could all dip into, like our own subconscious but one that served all humans. It seemed to me, a person who really wanted to be a storyteller, to be possibly like some kind of mainframe that – if we were lucky or particularly talented – we might be able to hack into in our dreamtime. From this collective well came not only our story structures but our archetypes too – kind of character types: the trickster, the hero, the witch and a whole host of others.

I delve deeper into the box and out comes Clarissa Pinkola Estés's book, *Women who Run with the Wolves*.[3] At last, a female author, and it's about wolves and women. This book surprised everyone and somehow hit the zeitgeist, proved by 145 weeks on *The New York Times* Best Seller list.

I had bought it but not read it. Clarissa herself turns out to be a Jungian analyst, which is possibly why she is in the same box as Jung and Campbell and probably how she had access to the mainframe. In her non-writing life she uses story and myths to help women on their life journey. I love the theory, which follows on from the work of Campbell and Jung, that she sums up so beautifully: 'Story is far older than the art and science of psychology and will always be the elder in the equation no matter how much time passes.' In short, stories are a chance to receive guidance for our soul, which perhaps I could do with right now. She encourages us to listen with 'soul-hearing'. Suddenly uncomfortable, I shift my position on the floor a little. I'm not so sure about soul-hearing. I have a flashback to a yoga studio.

I was meant to be doing a teacher training course but I just couldn't get into it. The anatomy stuff was fine. The actual yoga was brilliant. The teachers were phenomenal. But the chanting, the breathing, the sitting in silence, the 'soul stuff' . . . that bit was proving quite tricky for me, and there was an awful lot more of it than I had realised. The crunch point came when we were cross-legged, eyes closed, in silence apart from the sound of the teacher's voice telling us how and when to breathe. I was just desperately concentrating, wishing to see how my breath could take me 'deeper' into it. Over her relaxing tones, I heard the swish of a door opening but her hypnotic voice, although it faded a little, didn't miss a beat. What was she doing? *Breathe.* By my calculation, there was only really one door she could have opened. *Out, two three.* Suddenly, with the door left open, I could hear the tinkle of her having a little wee in the loo. As if nothing was occurring, all the while, she carried on in her hypnotic way: 'And slowly fill up your lungs again, right from the bottom, breathe in two three.'

I felt the absurdity so much more keenly than the relaxation. It bubbled within me, rising to the surface quicker than my breath. I couldn't help taking a chance and allowed one eye to open just a tiny bit. Through the chink, I peered around at the rest of the class. Surely it wasn't just me? It was. The others all had an expression of peaceful contentment that wouldn't be marred by a mere bodily function. How did they find it so easy to control the corners of their mouths? There wasn't a turn-up in sight, just soul-deep serenity.

I never did make it to yogi status. Still, maybe now is my chance to get soul deep; perhaps this is my time to discover the soulful woman within and what I have been missing. For me, a hybrid of scientist and storyteller, the promise of the science of story is a beautiful premise for a book. Surely I can rise above my own silly resistance to the soul stuff? Maybe, guided by Clarissa on a tour of myths and archetypes and wild women I will find that I simply embrace it?

Sadly the squirming continues. I'm just not the 'barefoot dancer cloaked in beads and feathers' type. I mean, I can be but it's likely to be a happy accident in front of a dressing-up box or too many rums on holiday rather than the deliberate search for some kind of spiritual communing. Clarissa's tour of the woman of myth is a fascinating one, however, and it includes that of *La Loba*, the wolf woman. Ah, now I could get with this programme. 'A healthy woman,' says Clarissa, 'is much like a wolf', with qualities of a 'strong life force, life-giving, territorially aware, inventive, loyal, roving.' Yes, Yes, Yes! 'Yet, separation from the wildling nature causes a woman's personality to become eager, thin, ghostly, spectral.'

Her book is about women who have lost their relationship with their wild self, which could be me, but there is no getting away from the fact that her take on the current 'female' situation is a spiritual one. In many ways, for her, the work of us women seems to be in re-excavating a wild spirit we have.

She relates the story of meeting a bone woman and says she has never been the same since. The bone woman is the heroine of the *La Loba* story and frankly, although I realise mine is a shallow opinion, she sounds about as far from 'attractive' as it gets. Anyhow, the bone woman/wolf woman is a loner – fat and hairy, living in the wilderness, cawing and cackling and making animal sounds. Her 'job' is to collect and preserve bones, especially those that could be lost. She spends the day scrabbling in the dirt, looking for old ones until she has found an entire skeleton. Her favourite type, her 'speciality', is wolf bones. She brings the bones back to her cave and, in the light from her fire, she then assembles the skeleton.

Well, I'm not sure if you have ever been on a fossil dig, but I have and I can tell you it isn't easy to find all the bones in a skeleton. The big ones can be obvious but there are lots of tiny ones to find too and many will have been spread about over a wide distance by foraging scavengers. Anyway, Clarissa doesn't mention that, and the wolf woman, after careful consideration, sings her chosen song over the skeleton. She raises her arms and that is when the magic happens. The rib and leg bones gain flesh and then, when all the flesh is there, the fur grows back. (There is no actual mention of the major organs, critical to biological functioning, but I'm assuming they are part of the flesh.) There is more singing and more reappearing until finally a breathing wolf appears before her. Ta-da!

But she doesn't stop there. She sings ever more deeply until the desert itself shakes and the wolf opens its eyes, jumps up and runs off. Then, as if that wasn't enough, as it runs off into the wilderness, the wolf is transformed into a laughing woman running free. You didn't see that coming, right? Neither did I.

So, off she runs into the vast beyond and that's where the story ends, but I'm curious now. Clarissa has me fired up to ask more. What happened to the woman? Did she stay wild, running through the desert, howling sweet nothings at the moon with not a care for the hardening of the skin on her feet, or did she just saunter into the next rustic desert town, steal a dress off a washing line and get a job in the local dime store? What, actually, is that story all about?

Of course that's the power of a good story: it gets us curious about ourselves and, in this case, about women, wild ones. Clarissa's own take on it is the story's promise 'that if we will sing the song, we can call up the psychic remains of the wild soul and sing her into vital shape again.' I remain uncertain about my own take on it, and certainly my own ability to do that, but, surrounded by my lifelong collection of wildlife, animal and conservation books, I might assume somewhere inside me is some kind of wild soul.

The archetype of the old woman is also common in mythology. She is the wisdom born of surviving and probably birthing many generations. Clarissa suggests there is an 'old one who knows' inside all women – we just have to connect with it. The wild woman described in *Women who Run with the Wolves* lives in a 'psychic kind of land'. Metaphorically she might run around in the desert but she's really in our souls. All this is kind of spacey and shape-shifty in a way that palaeoanthropology sometimes is when a new hominid is discovered.

There is much in her book I love. The way she says the spiritual lacerations of profoundly exploited women were referred to as 'nervous breakdowns'.[4] The way she describes the memory 'of our absolute, undeniable and irrevocable kinship with the wild feminine, a relationship which may have become ghostly from neglect, buried by over-domestication.'[5]

Something is calling me, especially the over-domestication bit, but – at the risk of upsetting Clarissa and offending her fans – I confess I'm left leaping and grasping in mid-air and then landing back down on science, my reassuring bedrock. Clarissa says 'over intellectualisation can obscure the patterns of the instinctual nature of women', which means I might be buggered but there are some thoughts floating around here, like dandelion heads that I want to keep an eye on as they take root.

What does it really mean to be a wild woman? What would we be if we weren't 'domesticated' and fettered by over-thinking and washing-up and men and relationships? The very thought is a little terrifying. The crone, the hag, the wrinkled, the (*gasp!*) unshaven, so in touch with her hidden wildness that she is acting out a little too much. While singing over bones in a deserted cave and bringing a wolf woman to life from the bleached white bones of death might seem magical, at the same time it's frankly pretty creepy. What is interesting to me, however, is passion, a lust for life, a connection and an intimate knowledge and understanding of wild things. Also strength, a determination, caring and understanding for something that is altogether way bigger than us. Those elements of the wild woman are what I'm inspired by.

What I get from Clarissa's book is that we fear being wild because to be wild would mean to be out of control, disgusting, not kind or gentle. So if I embrace this wild woman archetype, what would that mean? What would happen? Would my children be wading through the stinky plates and slimy dishcloths to find the sink just to drink a little water? Oh hang on, that already happened. Well, would they be waiting at the school gate while I gambolled around, being emotional in the brambles? Crikey, that almost happened too. At this rate they might eventually become feral. Oh wait . . .

Anyway, I don't want to write a book about children but an exploration of what kind of woman I'd like to be, what my relationship with the wild really is and what kind of wild women are really out there. I do know that I am happy in a way I can't quite find elsewhere when I am *out* out. It gives me something and makes me feel small, knowing that there is something far greater than me. For me, that greater thing isn't spirituality or religion, it is nature wherever that is to be found. Nature has a way of creating awe. Can I find that again?

If we are using women running with wolves as an analogy, here is what it might be for me. In the same way that an omega in the pack feels safe somehow because he is at the bottom, that is what nature makes me feel: it's bigger than me, it's better than me, and actually the way I evolved was to do my best to survive and grow and nurture my family within it. I wasn't evolved to obtain mastery of the natural world (as my garden will testify) but to witness it and work with it. And now that we humans have been stomping all over it for years, I'd like somehow to mitigate some damage.

The wild landscape has been dominated by men for so long, and I've discovered only two female archetypes: the woman as nurturer – think 'mother nature', 'mother of life', 'mother earth'– and the woman as a crazy crone who has never so much as touched a detangling spray, whose nails are dirty from grubbing for roots, who has a spiritual connection with plants and beasts and who seems to be so in touch with her 'wild' spirit that she is barely human.

Which one am I? Neither. The real freedom we have, surely is just to be whichever kind of wild woman we want and not sticking to anyone's idea of what a wild woman should be: flinging your knickers off after a good night out, or an old hag with bones, or Jane Goodall. If stories are the chance to receive guidance for our soul, then maybe stories are better than psychoanalysis, and maybe I need to seek some out. If I'm going to start revising who I am, maybe I need to go back to women who inspire my passion for the natural world and hear *their* stories and move forward to a life where that passion is flaming so bright that I forget to be depressed.

So, who are my non-mythical, non-goddessy real wild women? And what can I learn from them?

CHAPTER THREE

Memories – Scrambled
Brain Anyone?

My mind is a peculiar place at the moment, caught between worlds. I've gone back in time to a family home that I loved but thought I had left, and yet I haven't left it because it is now the future. The world has stood still because of Covid and yet it hasn't. My kids are growing and soon they will be gone, soon I won't be a wife or a mother in my day to day, and yet as I watch their confusion at being here and at our life now, I see they are still also boys. Back and forth goes time in the jumble of my head to a future unimagined, a past miscomprehended and a present where I don't really know who I am. What kind of woman am I now? What kind of woman was I before? What kind of woman did I want to be before all this life happened? What is a woman anyway?

All the while, this place reaches out to me. Inside are the endless boxes, unpacking and organising. Yet I yearn for the outside, which also calls me to repair and restore it, to explore it anew, to be the guardian that takes it through another generation just as I promised I would. In contrast to the chaos in my mind, it is calm, it is continuity, a response to the existential crisis I seem to have found myself in.

———

I'm perched on a small rock on a vast desert plain in South Africa.

'Can we find you anywhere more comfortable for that?'

'No thanks, I'm great here.'

I pause for a second, mirror in one hand, blusher brush in the other, looking up into the kind and bemused face of the tough, green–clad animal tracker beside me, his years in the wilderness not showing remotely on his smooth skin.

'Want some?'

I wave my blusher brush at him, he laughs and shakes his head, 'No, no, I don't want that.'

Really we are both laughing at the nonsense of applying make-up in the wilderness.

For me it was part of the job. Over the many years in TV, I got applying make-up for filming down to a slick art. Rather than blushing myself orange at silly o'clock in the pre-dawn under the fluorescent lights of a motel bathroom, I'd usually just find a spot in the daylight to sit and slap it on quickly while the crew were setting up their kit. That way, to me, make-up was just a presenter tool like batteries were a camera crew tool. I could apply it quickly anywhere – and often did. In fact, I quite liked my make-up moment; it was usually a good time between coats of mascara to glance around, take in our new location, and relish the sheer variety of my job at that time. From one day to the next I could be filming a rocket launch at NASA, examining cheese made from breast milk in a laboratory, or – like today – taking in the glory of a huge landscape. Although I got some funny looks, I liked the challenge of applying liquid eyeliner while bumping along a track in a 4x4, or getting to grips with the type of mascara that could cope with a whole day in the rainforest and not need retouching at all.

Make-up isn't usually what we think of when we think of a woman interested in conservation, is it? And what is that all about? It's as though, if you want to be taken seriously, you shouldn't wear make-up or care about it and you probably shouldn't have blonde hair – as though it might imply that you aren't taking your job seriously if you focus on looking good. Believe me, I have even tried being 'au naturel' for TV, surrounded by men who don't 'get it', but I learned the hard way: 'fake naturel' is what's required; otherwise when you have to watch yourself (an activity I detest) you deeply regret it. And comments like 'you look a bit peaky, were you ill that day?' don't help.

It's odd being a woman sometimes . . . but on this day I didn't care at all, I was just happy to be in the wilderness, making a film about rhino conservation. If I'm in the wilderness and there are no TV cameras around, my make-up bag stays at home. After all, making sure my make-up is OK and that I look good feels just a little trite when there are people getting down to the nitty-gritty of protecting globally vulnerable species and supporting equally vulnerable communities. So, a quick zip of the make-up bag and now I could turn my attention to the best of days ahead: we were setting off, on foot, for a day in the desert tracking wild rhino.

At that time, conservation projects were waking up to the idea that local people had invaluable skills and knowledge that could and should be used to protect globally valuable species. Nowadays, the idea that local communities are a critical part of conservation is a given; in fact, we have realised that conservation only works if local people feel inspired and empowered, and over and over we have learned that when a local community actually benefits from a conservation project then it becomes self-sustaining and of benefit for communities who often live in challenging economic circumstances. So, for this trip, funding had been provided for local expert animal trackers in South Africa as one way to help keep tabs on the extremely endangered Southern White Rhino and keep them safe.

We trekked for miles that day, through rocky outcrops and up hills, across wide sandy valleys. We saw tracks, and we even allowed ourselves to get excited, but we didn't see or film a rhino. That, my friends, is the reality of filming with wildlife – sometimes they don't get the memo. It was a shame for the film but still a day of being in that landscape, of pushing myself to keep going in the heat, appreciating the cracked dried ground and the plants that seized any opportunity to grow and adapt to their parched home, and a chance to wonder at how an experienced tracker could make sense of a scuff in the earth.

Years later I was to find myself back in the Great Karoo – this time as a mother with three children. I hadn't a clue where my make-up bag was but I definitely had eyes on a small plastic baby cheetah toy, originally named 'baby cheetarey'. Baby cheetarey had travelled with us around the world and had only got lost 1,537 times – on beaches, on planes, on a gravelled path where it was perfectly camouflaged (who knew cheetah-spotting could be so difficult?) – but so far, each time, the cheetah had been rescued and rediscovered with tears of relief.

One of my deepest joys at being a mother was not really spotting tiny plastic cheetahs in different habitats but showing my children the world. For the first time, I became an anxious traveller. It's one thing being buffeted through a thunderstorm in a small plane when it's just you, but when that plane contains all three of your children you suddenly discover anxiety that you never knew you had. Like instinctively knowing the importance of cheetarey's whereabouts, this was another, quite new, motherly instinct. However, after a long and slightly anxiety-inducing journey in a tiny plane – this time bumping over mountain thermals – the boys and I had landed on the flat and familiar plains of the Karoo and we were now in a safari truck, in a place that had long intrigued me; the Samara reserve.

Andre was our guide, and he had immediately captivated the boys. He looked like something out of an adventure story and scooped them up in a whirlwind of enthusiasm about all the important jobs he needed help with, like looking for wild animals. He was every boy's dream. After a short distance, he stopped the vehicle in a dried-up river bed and said in his South African accent: 'I think you'll like this.'

Lion, perhaps? Hyena? No, there would be none of those because they didn't exist here any more. Our first encounter was with ... tortoises – lots of them – gathering in this dusty place to mate. Quite unlike any other safari, to my initial shock, here the children were out of the vehicle in a trice, crouching around a tortoise with Andre, asking how many hundreds of years old it might be.

'Well, she is quite large so she might be quite old. This one is a female,' Andre told them as he demonstrated how she liked to be 'gently' stroked on the top of her head.

Absorbed as they were, I gazed around at the unassuming landscape and only then, when my eyes were tuned in, did I realise just how many pale-brown tortoises were around. A closer look also revealed quite a bit of bumping and grinding – very comical but I was unwilling to bring too much attention to that particular behaviour right now. My children were not really strangers to the concept as they had all been weaned on natural history films very early. In our house, David Attenborough rather than the Cartoon Network reigned the living room. However, it had recently become apparent that the actual details of mating weren't quite clear in their heads when, on the school run, we passed a couple snogging on the corner of the street and Gus announced loudly: 'Hey, look at those two mating.' The windows were all down at the time. Luckily the lights changed and I hit the gas. Anyhow, I felt that, for now, their understanding was probably age-appropriate.

Apparently, Andre went on to say, referring to some particularly boisterous tortoise action a little way away, we had to be careful because male tortoises can move quite aggressively if they choose and could quite happily run over a five-year-old. I remember wondering if it was bad for a mother to think she'd quite like to see that. I mean, compared to a gathering of small boys, how boisterous can a gathering of tortoises actually be? Andre recommended we move on before it got too hot. (I assumed he meant the river bed rather than the tortoise action.)

It was a joy to see this unfolding landscape not only through the wide eyes of the boys but also for myself. It was the story of Samara that had seduced me, so when I was asked to write about travelling with children in South Africa, I jumped at the chance to go there. At the time, the lodge had only been open to visitors for a few years because originally the Tompkins family had simply bought it for themselves as a place to retreat to, but that was not to last; Samara, like it or not, had come with a vision.

The Tompkins family had fallen in love with the property at first sight. They had been bewitched, not only by its immense sweeping beauty but by tales of what it had been. These valleys – now pretty desolate and bare of all the typical safari wildlife, like elephant, lion, leopard and hyena – had been, by all accounts, a land teeming with wildlife. Written descriptions from less than two hundred years ago speak of a place that was very different. Hunters and farmers encountered herds of millions of antelope, shoulder to shoulder for as far as the eye could see. There are accounts of a great springbok migration, following the rains in the same way that the famous wildebeest migration does through Kenya and Tanzania. In Lawrence G. Green's book, *Karoo*,[1] he describes a personal account from a farmer, Gert van der Merwe, of how these great herds could first be seen as a cloud of dust in the distance and how, moving at speed, the millions of animals would trample anything in their way. In fact, one of the descriptions vividly details a time when they did find themselves in the way. They survived.

The last time the migration was recorded was in 1896. The ancient path of this great migration soon became blocked by humans, as the landscape was divided by roads and fences, transformed by farms and towns. Not even millions of antelope could find their way through. As we drove around the empty landscape, I felt a great sense of a place waiting, waiting to be filled with life again. Perhaps Sarah Tompkins had discovered it at just the right time. She had already begun a long process to rewild it, but I wondered if, after so many decades of abuse, it was simply too late for this land.

We drove high up to the plateau, where we discovered a small group of just ten zebra, grazing on the high meadow against the backdrop of the wide valleys and escarpments. They raised their heads to stare at us before trotting away. Cape Mountain Zebra are different to their plains cousins, and there are only a few thousand left. They prefer rugged land to the lowland plains, they have a slightly different social structure and they carry their babies for twelve months, but they are most easily recognisable by the fact that their tummies are plain white with no stripes. This small group of wary individuals had not long arrived and had no sense of the significance of their presence here as the first Cape Mountain Zebra to start a herd on this plateau in decades. I remember vividly being thrilled to my core as I watched them trot away, the wind at their manes and tails. The very idea that you could go and purchase a herd of endangered zebra and bring them back to a place they belonged was deeply inspiring to me.

On the safari days that followed, we spent more time out of the jeep than in it, eyes glued to the ground. Once more I found myself in the Great Karoo checking for rhino tracks, but we also looked for giraffe and, most importantly, cheetah. There aren't many places where you can track cheetah on foot, but Samara is one of them. One morning we were up hours before the sun. When it finally rose, it found Fred, my oldest, cloaked in layers of oversized warm sweatshirts and looking like an extra from *Star Wars*, standing atop a Land Rover, his bright blond hair caught by the new sun's rays as they touched this high ground. He was holding a telemetry aerial as high as he possibly could. We were all quiet, listening for the reassuring *blip blip blip*s that would tell us whether Sibella, the collared cheetah we were tracking, was close by. Particularly special, Sibella was the first cheetah to walk this land in 130 years and we spent hours and hours looking for her.

Despite being the stuff of our living room nature documentaries and as familiar as the succulent on your nan's windowsill, as a species, cheetahs across the world have not had it easy. They once stalked prey in India, and humans – revering the big cat as a hunting companion – took them from the wild for hunting parties for the Maharajah and anyone who could afford them until, eventually, inevitably, there were no more left to take. The cheetah disappeared from India in 1956. In Africa, cheetah were also persecuted as wild land became farmland, habitat was lost and they were hunted. The 1960s and 70s saw the wild population plundered to fill our zoos, who were failing to breed them successfully in captivity. So, wanting an extra income, African farmers trapped cheetahs in their thousands. Zoos preferred females so any male who happened to find themselves trapped was surplus to requirements and usually killed. We humans have managed to drop the wild cheetah population from 100,000 in 1900 to just 7,100 today.

Sibella was a cheetah who would end up making history, yet hers was a distinctly dismal start. At less than two years old she almost lost her life to hunters. When she was discovered, she was in what seemed to be an utterly hopeless situation. Her back legs had been ripped to shreds by hunting dogs, she had been beaten, locked in a cage and she was gagged; her mouth was stuffed full of rope. It was here, by some miracle, that a wildlife charity found her close to death. She survived a five-hour surgery and then many, many hours of rehabilitation. Against the odds, she not only walked again but was offered the chance of a new home at Samara. In April 2004, she stepped out of an enclosure, going down in the history books as the first wild cheetah in the region for 130 years – a testimony to her sheer will to survive. Surviving in the wilderness would be her next challenge.

Just a few years later, our family tracked her progress through the land she had made her own. Although she remained elusive, none of our time was wasted: every day brought us something new as we familiarised ourselves with the lie of the land and the variety of habitats on it, from the sweeping and vast low plains of Camdeboo, to the ridges and cliffs and bluffs on the climb to the higher plateau. Even that bumpy drive held a tremor of excitement as Andre told us about rumours of leopard hanging around and instructed us to keep our eyes peeled.

At my request, we went to see an old ranch that the Tompkins had bought. There were eleven in all. Part of Sarah's plan was to buy out all the surrounding ranches that could no longer make a living because the land was too depleted. The owners were only too happy to sell. This ranch house had a weird atmosphere, as abandoned buildings do, and I was on the lookout for snakes as I entered the old, broken home now covered in weeds. I stood where a window had once been and looked out at the view, glorious yet empty. There was no glass, just a ripped fly screen. The hills in the distance blushed green and what garden there was had only a few trees to boast of; other than that, the land beyond the fence was just yellowing bush. I wondered for a moment about the owners – who they were, what their dreams had been in this remote place – but I didn't have much time for that because the kids were a bit bored and had started to poke around, looking for snakes.

Sarah's vision for this place was not only to protect as much land as possible, or even to merely conserve it, but actually to restore it to its former glory. I wasn't aware of the term rewilding in those days but this was to be rewilding on a grand scale: restoration of former wildlife corridors and, as much as possible, ancient migration routes.

We continued with our cheetah hunt. Two male cheetahs had been released in August 2004, four months after Sibella. In May the following year Sibella proudly showed off a litter of five healthy cubs. She had been inspired not just to survive but to thrive. By the late afternoon – when we finally got close enough to creep up, crouch down and see her sprawled out on her side, relaxing under some bushes in the warmth of the lowering sunshine – she had already begun to truly live the life that she deserved.

I watched my sons crouching in the bushes, peering at this incredible, resilient mother who had been through so much yet was tolerating their presence with no more than a glance at them, and the moment has never been lost on me.

CHAPTER FOUR

Spekboom to Rebloom

Now, a mother alone, I find myself hungry for the same kind of inspiration. For those stories of others with a similar genotype, the one that gave babies, grew breasts and delivered the unholy menopause just when you thought you were out of the woods. I want to reach back and forward to the women and the females of the wilderness. I need to remind myself of the value of belief and purpose.

Sibella's strength and resilience were only matched in Samara by Sarah's. Catching up with her, even after all these years of child-rearing and being wifely, finding out if her vision has become a reality, is suddenly important. She hears my news with sadness, expressing that Darwinian thought of 'it isn't the strongest of the species but the more adaptable that will survive,' and it is comforting to hear her slight South African twang once more.

My first questions are, of course, about Sibella. Although she no doubt suffered as a result of her injuries, her resilience changed the trajectory of her life: once out of her enclosure, she became perfectly capable of hunting not only for herself but also for her many subsequent litters of cubs. She turned out to be an amazing mum, giving birth to her cubs on steep slopes to keep them safe from predators and never eating before they had had their fill. She brought each new litter to meet her human protectors, which says something about how she must have overcome her fear of humans after the terrible way she had been treated. She was to live until September 2015 and in that time she had nineteen cubs spread over four litters, the last being when she was so old that no one thought she was capable of even getting pregnant again. Sibella was a supermum for a species that really needed it, and I can hear the pride in Sarah's voice as she

tells me she contributed to almost 3 per cent of the current
cheetah population in Africa. Her lineage now spreads across
fifteen protected areas in South Africa alone. She died
hunting as a wild cheetah. Her prey on that day was a very
small antelope called a duiker, which are pretty shy, live
mainly in the forest and have small but sharp horns. This
particular hunt would result in mortal wounds and, despite
the vet's best efforts, Sibella died of those wounds on the
operating table.

'Samara now has nine cheetah including some cubs,'
Sarah tells me. 'We like to keep the population as healthy as
possible, and Sibella's offspring have been sent to Malawi
and Zambia and other national parks. While there are
cheetah being sent back to India, we are not confident
enough to send any yet. The worry is that the habitat is still
too marginal.'

Restoring a species is not all plain sailing, and sometimes
female bravery is not enough, especially when it comes to
protecting young ones.

'We did lose one female cheetah to a lion recently. It was
an accident. She was hunting a springbok that ran into a
lion. She really should have retreated and she would have
been fine, but she had cubs and it was because she was
trying to protect them that she got killed.'

'But I guess that's part of living a wild life,' I say. Sarah is
quiet. I suspect the loss doesn't sit easily with her.

'There are now 7,100 cheetah in the world, so the number
has climbed a little bit, but there is still a way to go.'

'Tell me about Samara,' I say.

'Samara, as you know, was very much a passion-led
project. We immediately fell in love the minute we saw it. It
was just so beautiful. At first it was just going to be a family
home, but then it became obvious to me that there was a
much bigger project here. We started by putting together
blocks of land – the eleven ranches that were either
struggling or just not paying their way because the topsoil

was so depleted – then we approached scientists and said, "please come and guide us on our journey." Over the years we have had lots of different researchers on historical species. We have five of South Africa's nine semi-arid biomes, which only increased the idea that this would be our lifelong purpose and passion to restore species and downgraded land and restore skills. We didn't realise at the time just how important our position was. We sat at the nexus between these national parks and so we became the catalyst for change in the whole region.'

Sarah is talking about the Camdeboo National Park, Mountain Zebra National Park, Mount Camdeboo Game Reserve along with other protected game reserves and, to the south, a link with Addo Elephant National Park, the third-largest in the country, which could provide the potential to recreate and preserve old elephant migration routes. The possibilities are huge.

To begin with, Sarah was creating a huge mindset shift for the whole area, which – in order to preserve this amazing place – would need to go from small stock farming to encouraging wildlife, 'from wanting to kill animals and have trophies to allowing those animals to live and thrive in a habitat where they once roamed unabated.' The first of many hurdles concerned Sibella and her introduction.

'It was particularly challenging with cheetah, the first predator we introduced,' Sarah tells me. 'The challenges went back very far – this was the first time for 130 years that cheetah were walking the land. What we didn't know then was that the lions and elephant would be even more challenging. Our argument revolved around the fact that, if the prey base on the property was sufficient, there would be no need for them to predate other things. But our neighbours were worried and we had legal battles. Dealing with them meant negotiating with a certain type of mentality, so blinkered in vision that they couldn't see a balanced point of view. It was a battle of perception. We were only trying to restore what had historically been here. We sit in a really valuable biodiversity hot spot that could be lost for ever – an enormous threat to the world.

'Lion were really the major battle. It went on and on and sometimes seemed hopeless. Finally the Department of Environmental Affairs sent the permission through. One day, after years of work, an email just popped into my inbox and there was the permit for lion. I couldn't believe it! That was in 2018 and it was a massive day of celebrations. We released them in January 2019. Of course, it didn't all go completely to plan. Firstly, when they were in a period of adjustment where they were meant to be secure in the boma [enclosure] for a certain length of time, one – who clearly had his own agenda – escaped a little bit early. Everything was fine and we found him quite happy and feeding on a nice juicy warthog and completely unaware he had broken the rules. But we got there in the end, and the return of the apex predator changed everything – I mean *everything*. Changes we couldn't have predicted. The cheetah behaved differently. The Black wildebeest and Cape zebra, even in a time of drought, had even more young because there were more predators. It was extraordinary. Our jackal population – instead of behaving like predators, which they had been doing – have resorted to becoming scavengers again. The consequences to the whole system of introducing an apex predator are so far-reaching. It's a living, changing landscape and it will be extraordinary to see what happens next.

'We have even had leopard return naturally. Brown hyena need to come next. Farmers don't like them because they burrow under fences, but they are an important part of the natural ecosystem and the fences are not. Elephant were another big issue, of course, but again they are so important, they are the ecosystem engineers. There was definitely some resistance to us bringing them back, but we were looking at it as part of the stepping stones to a broader picture: that vision we have of Samara being a catalyst for change. We had the chance to create this corridor, to recreate ancient elephant migration routes from Addo up to the Karoo region.'

At first six elephants were released in November 2017 – a family group from the matriarch right down to the smallest female in the group. The matriarch, called Namkebo (meaning respect), was around twenty-five to thirty years old then and her calm character would be what enabled the small herd to settle in so well after such a big upheaval. It is never easy translocating elephants; they must be darted with tranquillisers and swiftly loaded into safe crates on big trucks, the sleeping group crane-lifted by their feet, which looks horribly dangerous but seems to be the safest and least harmful way. Then came the long drive from their Kwandwe Game Reserve on the Eastern Cape to their new home, Samara. At every step of the way the herd were monitored and taken care of.

Despite these efforts, elephant numbers are still decreasing in Africa as ivory poachers and habitat loss take their toll. For Sarah and her team, this only added to the reasons for such a difficult undertaking, providing elephants with a safe landscape, putting the species back where they belong.

'Watching that first female take her first steps out of the back of the truck and onto her new home was just really emotional,' Sarah says.

A year later, in November 2018, two six-ton bulls also made a huge journey, a twenty-four-hour drive from Phinda Game Reserve to Samara. Although the newly settled herd of females didn't exactly form a welcoming committee, the males found their feet, settled in and slowly made their presence known. By 2019 there was enough tracking evidence to indicate that some night-time liaisons were even occurring. The elephants are now tracked and observed;

where they go, where they drink, what they eat are all recorded.

'What we've seen is that they have taken Acacia thicket, which is really impenetrable and sometimes an invasive species, and they have turned that area into grassland, so it really is very exciting to see the effects of these species,' Sarah says.

'Then we have had a few curveballs,' she continues. 'Back in 2008, we were the first property targeted with fracking. We didn't even know what it was; no one had really heard of it then. We received a letter from our accountant to say that a company had applied for a licence to frack on the land. That they were looking for shale gas. We investigated and I called researchers all over the place to try to find out more about what it was. Some said "don't worry," others said "watch out for new techniques like this because they are invasive". So I employed a local lawyer and we managed to stop Bundu Gas. We discovered that they hadn't done due process or an Environmental Impact Assessment. Had we not fought that battle then, fracking would have gone ahead completely illegally and, more to the point, unregulated in South Africa. So now there is this protected environment of one million hectares of land in South Africa that is legally gazetted. Frackers can't come in unless the Minister of Environmental Affairs or the Minister of Energy gives permission. We have established a legal framework for conservation. There was some farming and some conservation land and I don't think I slept for six months trying to find all the different experts. Fracking was still such an unknown quantity. I had so many questions. When we were meeting with Bundu Gas, we asked what they would do with the chemical waste, and they said it was a company secret. This small company could easily have been sold to a bigger company like Falcon Oil or Shell, and the problem could have been bigger as a consequence.

'Activism is something we tend to do – because we have to. It is part of the job of protecting the place as we restore it, but not something I ever thought I'd be signing up for in those early days. We have so many stories; it hasn't been easy at all and there have been moments of great difficulty yet moments of great triumph – the return of the black rhino to the land, the bursting into bloom of the veldt and the pollinators and then of course the birds returning. We are at the coalface of conservation here and so there has been such a learning curve. As conservationist Doug Tompkins said, the key to climate control is restoration of land and so we follow and create as much best practice in that way as we can.'

Sarah tells me there are at least 1.5 million hectares of degraded land in the Eastern Cape and says, 'We have a spekboom planting programme.' She spells it out for me when it's clear I don't know what she means: 'S p e k b o o m – it's a plant. Native to the Eastern Cape. It's actually called *Portulacaria afra*. Spekboom is a local name. This plant is one of the gifts nature has up her sleeve, somewhat of a miracle plant when it comes to landscape restoration.'

The spekboom isn't particularly impressive to look at. A large succulent with reddish stems and small round green leaves, it looks like the kind of thing you might find in a dusty corner of the garden centre. In the wild, though, it is a heroine, a hardy semi-desert plant evolved to cope with the rigours and extremes of life in tough temperatures. Perhaps to its own cost, it is a great food source for animals, beloved by elephant, rhino, eland and kudu but also by goats and cattle, and so farmers allowed it to be overgrazed for many years and it practically disappeared. But there is big value in bringing it back. Once it's mature, which takes around ten years, the spekboom is a small tree around five metres high. It is drought- and fire-resistant, and it can provide shade and leaf litter to enrich the soil and a habitat for smaller shrubs to grow in. Its quick growth also prevents topsoil erosion, one of the core problems for the degraded land in the area. The plant's root structure binds the soil together, keeping it stable even in heavy downpours. This has all sorts of benefits, even helping to stop the rivers from silting up. It also seems to restore soil microbiology, benefiting the soil in all sorts of ways, speeding up the process from degraded to productive again.

In addition, one adaptation makes the spekboom slightly magical: this is one of only twenty-five plant species (that we know of) that can actually switch their photosynthesis methods according to the conditions. Photosynthesis is, of course, your regular everyday plant miracle; the process by which around 85 per cent of plants on our planet use water, sunlight and carbon dioxide to create the energy to grow and reproduce. In my garden, everything from a young oak tree to a wonky parsnip is at it. You might remember, from those biology book illustrations we all faithfully reproduced for homework, that most plants open stomata or 'pores' on the bottom of their leaves to absorb the carbon dioxide from the atmosphere. There's nothing extraordinary about that, and spekboom does this too in the wet periods; however, when conditions get dry it changes things up and actually closes the stomata during the day to save on evapotranspiration. If you are a plant, the downside of leaving your stomata open on a hot day is that you lose loads of water as it simply evaporates. But the spekboom has a way of dealing with this: when conditions are too dry, the spekboom only opens its stomata at night, and it switches to a kind of night-time photosynthesis method called CAM (Crassulacean Acid Metabolism). That means this plant is a carbon super sink. Measurements seem to indicate that it can absorb as much as 15.4 tonnes of carbon dioxide per hectare per year.

This fact has not gone unnoticed – the South African government is now running a programme as part of its 'working for ecosystems' project: to plant even more spekboom, to encourage landowners to do so, to employ people to do it and to create jobs where there are none. The aim is to restore 2.5 million acres using spekboom. There is talk among scientists and ecologists alike that this miracle plant can even affect the weather and, in the recent years of unparalleled drought, there is reason for optimism about that. Just by being present on the landscape, precious drops of rain, when they come, are absorbed into the soil, drawn up into the spekboom and the other plants it encourages, and evaporated out through the leaves, creating more water vapour in the air.

At Samara, Sarah tells me, every guest gets to nestle a spekboom cutting back into the land where it belongs, so that it can grow into a tree: 'They can understand the value of it and feel that even a small act is a contribution to rewilding this place.'

As to the future, Sarah tells me there are professors and other scientists working hard for the expansion of Addo Elephant Park.

'Between Graaff Reinet and the coast and the elephant reserve and us, the whole area is a three to four million hectare footprint of land that we are trying to create. And there is still that vision of the great African reserves coming together to create a network. But what is right in front of us now, and our focus for at least the next eighteen months, is helping the local community by tackling poverty. Without the local community we have nothing and we have to find ways to create long-term systemic change. Change that lasts hundreds of years, actually for ever, not just thirty or forty years. This is not like just throwing a sweet across a fence and saying "there you go, that should keep you going for a bit." This change needs to be permanent and we are trying to follow best practice in our region so that we can extrapolate that.'

I wanted to find inspiration and I have found it. Slightly awestruck by everything they have achieved at Samara since I was there in the early days, I tell Sarah that she is an amazing woman, and she laughs.

'We have big visions to protect the planet in whatever way we can,' she says. 'And of course it isn't just me, but I always say that women will save Africa. Women do everything, they are the nurturers but they are equally as able to deal with complex issues, they are much more rounded and more sentient on the whole. We women have a different approach, we are hard-working, we have that nurturing side that we have for our children and it can transfer to nurturing and caring for the planet in a way that men don't always have. That also helps when we are going into communities. As women, whatever we do – even if it is a small thing – we are saving the world one sure metre at a time. We've all got the ability to just do something. In fact,' she pauses for a second, 'we all have a *duty* to do something and the world has to wake up and recognise that. Just 4 to 6 per cent of global giving goes into the environment – it isn't enough.'

I know I'm feeling a little sorry for myself, acutely aware of my shortcomings, when I tentatively ask: 'Was it all plain sailing?'

'There were definitely hard times, and times when my husband wanted to sell and I had to claw and hang on to it. My intuition was clear to me; I think I was put on earth to do this and I had to hang on at all costs and there was no question for me.'

But the family have remained together and there is hope for the future, as Sarah proudly tells me of her daughters' work and investment in what they are creating at Samara and beyond. All that nurturing has meant that Isabella, their oldest daughter, is very much on board. As Sarah so delicately puts it, 'When I hit my pine box, Isabella is committed to the legacy. She is very involved in what we are doing and a great activist for the place. We are a living laboratory.'

CHAPTER FIVE

What I Can Do

It is time to look ahead. Rather than focusing on what I can't do, rather than listening to the negative voice in my head that has taken up residence of late, it is time to listen to the likes of Sarah and to see what I can do. To re-examine the visions of my own imagination from when I first became acquainted with this place I have called home for so long.

One of the things I value most here is the flood meadow. I value it because there isn't much left. Many flood meadows have been built on in our crowded island, but here we have a small patch that we have left to the wildlife. Unlike a regular wildflower meadow, which is nutrient poor, a flood meadow is rich and fertile because of the occasional dump of silt when the river breaks its banks and the high water table. Traditionally, flood meadows are used for grazing because of that fertility. I can't do that here but I can make sure it is taken care of in the right way, mown at the right time to reduce the invasive grass growth and give the flowering plants a chance.

Little by little over the years, this tactic has been working. The meadow is now home to wildflower species and insects, moths and butterflies, reptiles and small vertebrates that help feed the owls I hear at night and the sparrowhawk and kestrel I see by day. In the summer, where it was once just green grass – a monoculture really – now it is full of pollinators busy moving from one clump of flowers to another, trefoils, angelica, vetch and hawkbit, blues and yellows, whites and all shades of green. Gradually I was getting better at recognising the species but now, after so long away, I seem to have forgotten them all.

One cold morning as autumn is contemplating the turn to winter, I take my coffee and wander round the meadow. I see that in my own way I have already done something. The oak I planted at the far end of the paddock when my dad

recovered from cancer has grown into a sprightly and
beautifully round young tree. The gathering of silver birch
that were mere baby saplings now reach high and shimmer
golden, and tall seed heads draped with twinkling cobwebs
are left for the winter, providing not only grace and beauty
but also seeds for the coming seasons.

What hasn't done so well in the time I have been gone is
the pond. Once home to our otter, Honey, now the neglect
is showing. I had planted willow, and alder and hazel have
sprouted up too. I had sown wildflower seeds on the banks
and planted golden flag iris in the shallow boggy parts, but
in our absence the pond has silted up, the willows and alders
have overcrowded it, branches have fallen across and in it,
and the water is stale and the rotting leaves stink. This is not
meant to be a perfect part of the garden, by any means – in
fact, it is meant to be wild – but it could definitely do with
a helping hand.

I spend the rest of the weekend in waders and an old
t-shirt, armed with a pump, a shovel and a chainsaw, waging
war. I am soon joined by a son with a kayak, who paddles
under the undergrowth and floats branches back into my
reach so that I can drag them out of the pond. Between us,
we manage to clear the water of the fallen tree trunks and
slowly work our way around the edges of the water,
coppicing all the overgrown alder and hazel. By the time we
have finished we have a huge pile of branches. I will come
back and chop the biggest ones, stacking them in piles for
creatures to live in while they wait to be used for firewood.
We twist and tidy the willow fence back into place and we
pump the filthy water away. Then I dig out as much silt as I
can move alone because by now the novelty has worn off
and the kayak captain has gone inside to do less worthy
things with screens, leaving the disgusting job of clearing
the gunk to me.

Clearing the banks of weeds and the crazy spreading
alders has left space for wildflowers to grow again in the

spring, now that the light can get in once more. It was never going to be perfect, but it is better – and here I am, doing it 'one sure metre at a time'. Making change happen even if I do look like a wreck and I have discovered a hole in my waders. Even if I do stink and my back is killing me, I am doing it. At the end of the afternoon, I trail back to the house feeling – for the first time in a long time – just a little bit less of a loser.

That night I listen to the Tawny Owls screeching at each other. They really can make a terrible racket sometimes when you are trying to sleep, but still I am comforted to know they have somewhere local to catch dinner.

CHAPTER SIX

Perseverance

We all bring something different to the world of conservation, but do women bring something to the table that men don't? I find those last comments from Sarah really sticking in my mind. For me, my ability to tell the story helps a little, perhaps, but we all show up with a unique set of skills and experiences that influence what we bring to making the world a better place. Women are often accused of being too emotional for work that is physically and mentally tough, yet our emotional experience can also bring us to purpose, and to empathy and understanding. An awful event or situation can bring a new dream that begins to ease the pain and sometimes ends in a new reality.

When I was first visiting the conservation project leading the way in South Africa, not too far away in Zimbabwe a smart young girl called Nyaradzu Hoto was just beginning her school career. She was the sixth child in a family of eight children, growing up in a rural African village. In a Christian community she learned the difference between right and wrong, between cruelty and kindness. Her family were poor, things were very tough for them growing up and they struggled, but she remembers they were happy.

'My father was a ranger,' she tells me. 'He had a passion for it, and one day I remember the bucket was full of water and he helped an ant out of it to save its life because it was struggling to stay floating in the water. I remember laughing. To me, a child, it was very funny because ants are so small, but now I understand the meaning of it.'

Nyaradzu wears no make-up. Her skin glows with something else. Her hair is shaved short to her head, exposing the strong structure of her face. It has taken me a while to track her down but, being more and more interested in the world of women who work in the wilderness, I really wanted to hear her story.

When she was a child watching her father, his work as a ranger was not something she aspired to: 'I just saw that environment was dominated by men. I only saw that could be done by men,' she tells me.

'Regardless of pride, my parents didn't have enough money for me to continue with education,' she says. 'In desperation, I chose marriage at twenty; otherwise how would I survive? I thought my husband would be helpful and believe in me and support me in an education. I would be someone in life that would believe in the good spirit of all that, but sometimes life doesn't bring you what you hope. He wasn't supportive, he didn't allow me to fulfil my dreams. Everything about me was not valid. At the time I used to do all the labour for the whole family; there was nothing in my life, it was just to serve him. Sometimes I wished I could be a dignified woman with a career and helping to build a good life with my husband, but it wasn't like that. He was very violent. I felt myself that it was impossible. I saw it as an imprisoning life. Sometimes in life you need more learning. I didn't realise my marriage would bring an empty life. In a dark time you realise there is no option but to move forward or lay down and die.'

Nyaradzu found herself with a daughter, a husband who was an abusive, violent drunk, and his family – now hers – who saw her as a commodity and treated her as a slave rather than embracing her as a person, their daughter-in-law. She endured a lot, but in her culture women were seen as second-class citizens, domestic abuse was a given, and divorce was something only men did to women. To leave didn't seem to be an option because what would she leave for? If independence is removed from a person they are sometimes forced to rely on bullies and drunks. Yet some women have a strong voice inside, stronger than the voices of the world around them.

'What did you do? How did you change things?' I ask.

'Don't force yourself to stay in an abusive relationship,' she says. 'It was harder to stay than to go. I went to build up courage and divorce him. It was difficult for me, it was painful.'

Nyaradzu's voice still weakens as she describes the slow process of making her decision. The pain is clearly still there. Often, when we set off into a dark wilderness simply guided by an inner compass, a crazy hope that there is a path there somewhere, we find that those first tenuous steps taken in faith are what help us discover a path that leads to a whole new world.

'I told myself that nothing good goes easy,' she says. 'I needed to take a step forward to shift my life. My own father died and I left, and for three years I managed to sustain my family's daily living with gardening. But then, in 2018, a once-in-a-lifetime breakthrough came.'

Nyaradzu saw an advert in her local community centre, asking women who were interested to apply for the world's first all-female armed anti-poaching force. It's easy to say that all she had to do was show up and show them what she was made of, but the reality was very different.

This is where Nyaradzu's life journey intersected with Damien Mander's. They couldn't have been more different. Until now, Damien's life had been consumed by being a soldier at the top of his game. His childhood had one fear, 'that he would grow up without courage'. He served as a clearance diver for the Australian navy (the equivalent of the American Seals), and as a special operations sniper. While he was deployed in Iraq, he project-managed the Iraq Special Police Training Academy, overseeing training for up to 700 cadets, and after three years on the frontline of the Iraq war he departed in 2008 without a clue as to what he would do next. So he travelled, and in Zimbabwe he found his next mission.

In the middle of the bush, he and his guide came across a huge bull elephant with its face cut away. That elephant was the victim of poachers, and Damien confronted 'a deep sadness for an innocent creature'. It was a moment that changed him – the turning point, inspiration and motivation that he needed. He asked himself if, after all the courage he had already shown, would he now have the courage to save animals, and to give up everything his life had been so far in order to do so. He describes it as bouncing: 'When I hit rock bottom, I was lucky, I bounced.'

Damien went home to Australia and sold everything – every single personal asset – to found the International Anti-Poaching Foundation (IAPF). His plan was to use his hard-won military expertise in the 'on the ground' battle with poachers. Yet Damien had been at war for a long time, and he knew he didn't want to go there again, so the question he found himself asking was: 'How do we find a way to have a long-term good relationship with the community and not war?'

As well as his experience with the elephant, another very important thing had made an impact on him during his travels: 'When I first moved to Zimbabwe, one thing really struck me – it had the lowest life expectancy for women.'

Damien decided that the IAPF would create opportunities for the most marginalised in society, putting women at the centre of their conservation strategy. The more he followed that path, the more he realised it was a 'no-brainer'.

'The world is waking up to climate change,' he says, 'but I am one story in an overwhelming body of evidence that says empowering women is the answer.'

There were eighty-seven women in the first selection, and they were all survivors of sexual assault, domestic violence, AIDS orphans, single mothers and abandoned wives, but 'they are the bridge that brings communities together'.

Damien realised that winning the hearts and minds of local communities would be more effective than bigger fences and more guns. And so an all-female anti-poaching force – Akashinga or 'the brave ones' – was born.

'When spirit and character meet purpose, nothing can stand in a person's way,' Damien says. And when she attended a try-out, Damien met Nyaradzu – a woman he now describes, in his delicate Australian accent, as 'a fucking rock star'. Like all the women who sign up for Akashinga, she was greeted with hardcore marine training – not a 'soft' version, not a modified version, but one that will test their physical endurance and stamina and self-assertion to the point of growth.

'To become a ranger you have to become physically and mentally fit,' Nyaradzu tells me. 'You have to be strong and you have to be dedicated to it because even if it becomes too hard you will never give up. I knew I have to become someone else, so I have to work so hard. To me the running was the hardest part because the terrain was not good and I was not used to running. We used to run 5K and do push-ups, sit-ups, burpees.'

Nyaradzu has a great way of playing things down – she doesn't even mention the brutality of the midday African sun, and presumably there wasn't much time for sitting about on a rock and putting your make-up on as I had done before my delicate dalliance across the wilderness of South Africa. The training is tough mentally too.

'Damien helped us to use our spirit of hard working for changing things, breaking down barriers and challenges. He led us to become more strong and encouraged us that, if we join our hands together, as women we can change the world and change the story for wildlife. And I understand that women can be better rangers than men. Women can change the world if we are given the opportunity, and we can even do more than we think we can.'

'What is it in women?' I ask her. 'Where do you think the power lies?'

'Women naturally are teachers and that element you cannot easily find in men. Also, I realised that women are not easily convinced or easily bribed. Men are, but we women we cannot be, for sure.' Nyaradzu speaks of a sector of our world blighted by scandal and corruption when it comes to the poaching of animals and the sale and export of their parts: 'Also, in spending our salaries, women are better than men. We can spend most of our salary on our family as compared to men.'

It's not just the women who get a paradigm shift: 'The communities are now understanding that women can also be rangers. At first they were not understanding that men can be arrested by women but, because we had received the right training, we are strong enough and we encourage each other.'

Once she graduated training, life didn't stop being tough, but Nyaradzu now had the meaning and purpose she craved. Rangers spend most days patrolling on foot, covering a wide area and looking for signs of poaching activities. They monitor wildlife movement and collect data, recording all sightings and signs – 'we are already seeing that there is a big increase in wildlife' – and they remove snares and monitor water sources. If there are signs they follow up on poaching activities.

'We change the patterns of our patrols so poachers will not understand how we do it. We also educate people about our job and why we do it and teach people how to live in harmony with nature, to come up with solutions to human wildlife conflict.

'I have a strong bond with the animals I look after. Watching the elephants means life to me. I've come to realise that I have chosen the conservation centre as my best home. In the bush I'm thinking about the water source or where the animals are. I think in a way that is different – I know where to see the elephant or the water buffalo, and if I don't see them I think "are they OK?" When I don't see them it brings more questions to me. I love my elephants like my children.'

In that phrase is something that I think is the most primal thing I have ever experienced and over which Nyaradzu and I have an immediate understanding: the ferocity and power of 'mother love'. Damien is quite honest about how he is tapping in to women's natural instinct and drive to protect, something that has nothing to do with cultural limitations or 'can we?' but is just what we naturally bring to the world as females.

When I ask Nyaradzu what was it like the first time she came across poachers, she says, 'To me it was an opportunity to prove myself. I said that "I can do this job, we have to catch them".'

I ask if she has encountered much violence, and she says 'no' then pauses for a moment.

'I think it is because of the approach that we deliver. The approach of men is different to the approach that women do. Men sometimes are very harsh, they quickly come to a conclusion. We can assess the situation and de-escalate tension. We take it as an opportunity to educate them. They listen because maybe we are not so harsh by nature, we are teachers, we educate not accuse.'

Again, this could be mistaken for a soft approach, but poachers still get consequences for illegal activity.

'We don't threaten but lead them to understand why they are being arrested and what to do next. We haven't fired a single shot in all the arrests we have made.'

Akashinga are policing their own communities. They take part in door-to-door raids and they have taken down whole networks of poachers. The president's daughter has even volunteered to become a ranger.

Empowerment is a much-used word but, for Akashinga women, it is a new life force, a changing attitude that doesn't begin and end with a uniform and the ability to arrest poachers.

'Just before I was promoted to an Akashinga ranger leader,' Nyaradzu says, 'I went on after my training to acquire a driver's licence in 2019. It is a big deal for women.

'I just saw men being leaders when I grew up, and now I am a woman leader it means a lot to me. I am learning to be a wildlife conservation leader. In December this year I will be writing my final examination of my degree in conservation. I dream of bringing greater change to Akashinga and the rangers here, and in conservation management a greater understanding and to come up with solutions to the problems we will be facing with our communities. I dream to pursue maybe being in America or other countries so I can appreciate wildlife management in other countries. Perhaps I can be a role model to women in the world, raising a flag to Akashinga. I am strong today because I have been weak. I am fearless today because I have been afraid. And now I can fly. We have to fight for the natural heritage we have in Africa.'

The IAPF is now able to invest the same amount into the community every thirty-four days that trophy hunting in the same area could bring in per annum. The programme, which started as security providers for elephant and rhino, now leases its own land, and has moved from focusing on single species to biodiversity and expanded from just parks to open landscapes. The programme is growing, with a long-term vision for protecting wildlife sustainably. By 2026 the aim is that twenty reserves will be protected by a staff of 1,000 trained women.

'Trying to balance is tough but it is better than it was. My daughter is at school so much of her time and she stays with my sister when I am on patrol, and I am very happy how she is going now. She loves wildlife and maybe she will become a ranger too, but she is only nine so it is a bit early to know that yet. My passion only developed in Akashinga when I started to realise the importance of wildlife and imagining all the good works my father would do as I grew up. He passed in 2014. I wish he would have seen me become a ranger.'

By the way, in case you were wondering, Nyaradzu means 'perseverance'.

CHAPTER SEVEN

The Groundwork

This house, I discovered when I examined the deeds, had a strip of land called the donkey paddock running alongside the river. I wondered how many donkeys had actually lived there and for how long. Surely it must have been for a while for the small area to be called that. I also wondered if it meant the ground might still be a little fertile. The donkey paddock was right next to the river and you had to cross a little stream to get to it. It was, I had decided, the perfect place for an allotment.

The first seeds of a love of growing my own started with herbs. A fascination for the rich and delicate scents, for the mysterious and magical properties later turned into wonder at what fresh herbs cut from just outside my door could do to a cheese omelette or a chicken breast. It wasn't long before I was branching out into salad and then veg, but there was something else I loved: that soil-deep ability to sustain ourselves. Where did that come from? Like Nyaradzu watching her father with the ant in a bucket, I realised, the seed had been planted long before I got into herbs.

My mum grew up during the Second World War, deep in the countryside on a rural estate. Gardening, growing, and sharing produce were all as natural a way of feeding a family as a visit to a massive supermarket is for us. Later in life, her allotment became her 'me time' – the community, the veg chat, the digging and planting. While we were at school, she was at the allotment, tanned and slim, productive, self-sufficient. After school, we would go there.

'Where are your shoes?'

'Off.'

I remember the slip of the muddy bank, the cool rise of the water up my ankles, the slight tremor about the rumour of a giant lurking pike. I remember sinking the watering can into the river slowly until the water slipped over its rim and

sunk it, then the slopping walk back along the green
trimmed paths.

Deeply curious about each plot I passed, I could never
pay enough attention to the watering can, although I was
dimly aware that it got lighter and lighter the further up the
path I travelled. Each plot was, to me, surely a reflection of
each person who created it. I was and still am endlessly
fascinated by the way these regular rectangles were crafted
by irregular people. Each unique. Yet there was a timelessness
to them too – something I sensed in my mother. Something
that seemed reassuring.

There would be neatly tied wigwams of runner bean
poles, at first with trails of green snaking up, aiming towards
the top. By the time the days were hot and many more trips
to the river with the watering can were required in an
evening, those poles were laden with green and with long
beans that could barely be ignored for fear they would go
tough if they weren't picked on time. (A genuine fear
because those stringy beans made me gag.) Those with a
plot furthest from the river had wheeled trolleys stacked
with watering cans. Sometimes I wished our plot was a
little further away so that we could have one of those
trolleys.

The best evenings came later in the summer. One man,
who had an allotment in the prime spot practically alongside
the river, had a huge plot. It was at least three times the size
of ours and you could tell right away that it had been his for
many years. He had at least two sheds and lots of what at the
time seemed to me to be big trees and plants but were
probably a few fruit trees and bushes. He also had a
mysterious, large, square black room. Now I know it was a
fruit cage. I never actually spoke to him – he wasn't
unfriendly but I was very shy back then – but for two weeks
a year every summer, he was gone. And, in exchange for
keeping his allotment watered, which wasn't so hard
considering how close it was to the river, we were allowed

to go into the black room on our own. We only had to remember to always shut the door behind us. That was very important.

Once inside, we were surrounded by raspberry plants. I remember them being taller than me. And we were allowed to eat or pick as many as we wanted. At that time, to a little girl, it felt like being invited into Aladdin's cave and picking out the jewels. Every evening I would eat as many as I could and the following evening they would have all grown back. Magic.

I found myself somehow replicating this as a grown-up. One high-summer holiday morning, all laziness and lack of schedule, I threw open the doors and said to the kids, 'Your breakfast is in the raspberry and strawberry patch. You just have to find it.' There are moments when you feel that you got it right as a parent and that happened to be one. They ran off whooping and hollering because being given permission to be feral is all you need when you are a young boy – and of course each of them needed to be the first there. I sat and drank my coffee, listening and watching as they discovered each 'jewel'.

'Pick your own breakfast' went down particularly well for a while – a handy way to cut out the middle woman, who got a little moment to sit still and drink coffee – but there were many times when the whole allotment thing got too much. It seems a recurrent theme in my life that I take on too much and then end up overwhelmed and utterly frustrated with myself for not being able to achieve the impossible – perfection. 'Why not do twenty things badly when you could do one well?' appeared to be my motto even though I didn't ever choose it, and most of my life seemed to be a negotiation between dreams and visions and time and energy. So it was with the garden.

Little by little, over the next few years, one small square of dug-up land turned into two, then three, then another for all the different types of potatoes to last us through the different seasons. A small second-hand greenhouse found a new home here and some black, white and redcurrant bushes. They were closely followed by a few apple trees and a little quince and, before I knew it, I had a full-time job on my hands.

One afternoon I almost burst into tears because I couldn't keep up with the courgettes. I couldn't use them quickly enough or give them away because everyone had grown tons of courgettes and I had already frozen enough ratatouille to last us a decade. I realised how utterly ridiculous it was and, after I had got it out of my system, I stood in the garden having a good long think. The facts – the realities of time – meant that I couldn't possibly keep up with the weeds or the cooking, preserving, pickling or even picking of the harvest and work full-time and look after three boys. I had to remember I was not the entire staff of Downton Abbey, I was simply a working mother.

I contemplated the point of the garden. Financially, if you did the maths, these vegetables were probably more expensive than the freshest fruit and veg available at Harvey Nichols' luxury foodmarket. Did it give me joy? Well, it wasn't exactly relaxing to be welling up at the sight of a few courgettes.

'This is nonsense,' I told myself and resolved to take a break from it next year. It had simply got out of hand.

At that precise moment, Gus shouted: 'Mum.'

'Yes, I'm here.'

'Where?'

'In the garden.'

He ran up to me, clutching an enormous light sabre belonging to his brother. He must have realised I was deep in thought because he stopped quietly next to me and his eyes followed mine.

'Broad beans are doing well,' he said. 'Anyway we are playing Star Wars and going to eat biscuits now and I'm allowed to borrow Fred's light sabre.' And off he ran.

With that knowledgeable phrase about broad beans from such a tiny person, I was duly shown 'the point of it' and committed to at least another few years of hard labour. Now I have my doubts as to whether Gus would recognise a broad bean plant if one whacked him with a light sabre, but perhaps these inputs when we are young are the equivalent of planting some kind of seed. Just like Nyaradzu and the ant, or me and the raspberries.

The vegetable garden wasn't given much attention while we were gone. In fact, I'm sure our tenants never set foot in it. My potting shed, which I had happily painted forget-me-not blue, has been forgotten, its homemade bench and plastic window looking onto the stream both collapsed and covered in weeds. Rather than the rampant vicar rose that climbed over the roof, now a broken branch sticks out of it, letting in the water. The floor has rotted, the window slipped. The neatly organised pots and seed trays are still in there somewhere, but it is impossible to see them for tins of old paint, oil cans and tarpaulins, garden rubbish and spare parts for who knows what. On my first foray inside, I had tripped over a rat that – startled by my intrusion into his recently acquired family manor – had been trying to leave.

The greenhouse is no better. I never got round to doing the floor properly, and now it is filled with lanky weeds surprised by the extra height given them by the extra heat. Despite our gardener Ed's best efforts to get things back under control in our absence, once he had arrived, his hours were limited. And, with no one to eat the vegetables anyway, my vegetable beds filled with grass.

I decide on a new approach for a new era: raised beds. With the help of my friend Yasmin and little Gus, we spend a rainy Saturday building raised beds out of old scaffold planks. Screwing them together in position is the easy bit. Filling them is a different task altogether.

The irony is not lost on me. My neighbours have rescue donkeys. We hear them often, their strange calls echoing over the valley from time to time. Other than that, they are just comical and simply eat or observe us with their slightly woeful faces. They also produce wonderful manure, and I am welcome to help myself from the large pile. It is the perfect stuff for growing veg in. Over the course of a weekend, I shovel and wheel barrow after barrow – I lose count after twenty – of donkey manure back to the 'donkey paddock', rediscovering my shoulder muscles in the process.

Another job has been lurking outside. At the back of the house, leaves have built up over the seasons, leaving me with blocked drains but also with piles of rotted leaf mould – another nice source of nutrients for veg. So out come the shovel and the barrow again and, with Yasmin's help, at least another ten barrowloads. A little bit of topsoil added, then a good mix of the worm-filled lot, and the beds are filled.

After all that is done, I build a seat with some old bricks and a plank. It is with a strong sense of déjà vu, optimism and 'this time it will be different' that I sit on it, drinking coffee in the weak autumn sunshine, and open a seed catalogue.

WINTER

CHAPTER EIGHT

Clearing the Way

The tree has come down across the river.

High waters in the flurry of autumn storms have carved away at the bank, washing the soil from its roots till it could hold on no longer. It isn't the only tree down, but the other one is the size of a cathedral pillar and unreachable. Also it is higher and so won't provide too much obstruction when it is time for the waters to rise again.

Our river is responsive. Its ups and downs are a constant reaction to the amount of rain. It is usually predictable. If it is raining on the hills, it won't be many hours before the river levels rise, the water falling over the weir and frothing its way down to the village.

Today the water is low but this tree is a pain. It is slung low, right across the river, and I need to do something about it before it clogs everything up. And hey, I could do with as much wood as I can get for the wood-burner, which is merrily burning logs as if I have an inexhaustible supply.

After years of being told not to try to handle the chainsaw, it is a relief now to just get on with chopping logs whenever I want and to get the job done. In fact, I can't really understand why, throughout my married years, I never just picked up a chainsaw and ignored all 'well-meaning' advice to the contrary.

The day is bright, the river clear and shallow. The bottom of it here is sandy and smooth, really very inviting for a swim if this tree wasn't in the way and it wasn't the perishing temperature of early winter. I clamber down into the water and am about to start when I notice something in the sand just above the water level: otter prints. Two sets, one big and one small. Guaranteed to put a grin on my face.

The thing with trees is that they are much bigger than you think, and I never really learn. With the first cut a whole branch comes down right across the vegetable garden and into the opposite hedge, narrowly missing me. There is a saying that if a tree falls in the woods and no one hears it . . . Well, something like that. Anyhow, no one saw it nearly take my head off and that is the important thing.

It takes an afternoon, my wellies filled with water, but I get a few barrowloads of logs out of it and the river is cleared again.

CHAPTER NINE

Woodswoman

All this chainsaw action has reminded me of a long-forgotten book. An inspiration to me. Perhaps it is time to unpack a few more books. Anne LaBastille's *Woodswoman* promptly steals an afternoon by the wood-burning stove.

While they were being educated in the States, my boys had been exposed to the words of Henry David Thoreau rather than those of Jane Austen. Even though my first degree was in English literature, I knew nothing much about him but – on finding he was a naturalist who had written *Walden* about his experimental 'simple', 'back-to-basics' life in the woods – I had thoroughly approved. This, I felt, was a much more interesting education than Jane Austen. In my humble and perhaps slightly controversial opinion, the only good thing about Jane Austen was Mr Darcy. However, much as I approved of my sons studying Thoreau, I quietly noted to myself that I didn't hear any mention of them learning about Anne LaBastille.

Anne LaBastille was a pioneer in many ways. Growing up in a time when the most a girl could expect from her career was a decent job behind a desk, Anne tended to find her own path. 'You can't do that' didn't appear to be in her vocabulary. Born in New York in 1933, she was to spend her life escaping the confines of the city and, ultimately, to take that to extremes. Anne was an outdoors woman and a female conservationist in an era when neither was particularly welcomed or even considered feasible. Undaunted, she was only the second female wildlife major to study at Cornell University. Yet, when she left university, she learned that her gender meant she was unable to have an outdoor job, which made no sense to her at all and to us now is just laughable. This was to be a constant battle during her early career years. Her first conservation job was for the Audubon Society in Florida, launching herself from the 'behind the desk' starting line. After much persistence, she finally got her job in the field and even got the uniform changed from a skirt to much more practical trousers. She also got to publish her work in an outdoor magazine, although she had to use a man's name to do so. She did her PhD on 'The Life History, Ecology and Management of the Giant Pied-Billed Grebe' in 1969 at Colorado because that was the only university to allow a woman to work in the field, and she ran the first eco-tours out of the US to Latin America and the Caribbean with her husband until they got divorced.

And that was when – feeling utterly lost in life, desperate for peace and a home to call her own – Anne found a piece of land, miles from anywhere on a lake in the Adirondack wilderness, and she built herself a log cabin and wrote her book *Woodswoman*. Now I read it with fresh eyes.

'I hoped,' she wrote, 'that a withdrawal to the peace of nature might remedy my despair. I reasoned that the companionship of wild animals and local outdoor people could cure my sorrow. Most of all, I felt that the creation of a rustic cabin would be the solution to my homelessness.'[1]

The Adirondacks, the land neighbouring Anne's new home, is six million acres of forests and lakes, surrounding the Adirondack mountain range in New York State. Roamed by bears and deer, squirrels and beavers, it was protected in 1895 as Forever Wild in a precursor to the Wilderness Act of 1964, which went on to protect so much more federal land in the States. Her descriptions of her new home resonated with me so much, reminding me of Wyoming and the national parks there. The thing is, she may be a little tougher than me. If I were moving to a log cabin in the middle of nowhere, some of the things I might consider would be prowlers, bears, the idea that no one could hear you if you screamed, broken legs or worse, freezing to death or falling into the lake and freezing to death, loneliness. She does consider these things, but then buys a plot of land with no road to it. Whereas the rest of us might consider those fears perfectly sensible and so head back to a regular house with neighbours and central heating, Anne simply calls them 'silly spectral thoughts' and goes off in her boat to float a load of logs down to the site of her house, herding them like swimming sheep before whipping up a country cottage in no time in much the same way as they did in *The Little House on the Prairie*. Her drive to self-sufficiency has her designing a gravity-fed water system for the house, buying a gasoline pump to pump water from the lake to a tank on a high knoll above the cabin and then fixing plastic tubing to plumb it in as her supply.

Anne is no fair-weather cabin girl. She lives there year-round. In summer she swims in the lake sometimes two or three times a day, and she chops her own wood for fuel to keep the wood-burner in her cottage going for cooking and heat. The only way in and out of the cabin is by boat, so in winter she finally concedes to getting a snowmobile because the lake freezes and without it she has to walk all the way up the lake to get to her car. It eventually dawns on her that this is a precarious position to be in.

She fishes, she explores, she writes and hosts guests and – though sometimes lonely – when offered the chance to move in with a lover, she turns him down because she could not bear to leave this life she has created: 'In a world where millions upon millions of people live in cities and suburbs, owning nothing, renting out a tiny space in which they live out their lives, I feel that having our own land is a priceless gift.'

Her challenge to herself – to build her own house in the wilderness and live in it alone – was an interesting one just because she was a woman and it seems so unusual for a woman to do that. Throughout her life, she had already shown that she was no respecter of preordained gender roles, so why should now be any different? Yet she does concede that it is different for a woman and that what she is doing is unusual. Should we want to do the same, she gives us a little insight: 'The first thing was to convince myself that I could handle anything I had or wanted to . . . I believe a woman can do whatever she sets her mind to once she has learned how.'

Her love affair with the natural world shines through this book as familiar to me as if I had written it myself, and in so many ways reading her book again is like meeting a friend. We have a lot in common: she knows sorrow and she keeps a 16-gauge shotgun loaded at the door . . . OK, not that last bit. The only thing we don't have in common is that she is a tree-hugger. I know, it is rather unfortunate but I can forgive her for it. She is a literal tree-hugger. Like me, she does have her favourites but I do not hug mine. Anne describes a tree hug 'as though the tree was pouring its life force into my body. When I stepped away from the white pine I had the definite feeling that we had exchanged some form of life energy. This feeling seemed concentrated between my belly and breasts.'

Anne died on 1 July 2011 but she left an extraordinary legacy for someone who lived a 'hermit' lifestyle for so much of her life. She was an activist and a role model. She broke boundaries in the world of conservation for women, enabling future generations to take their place both in the world of academia and in the field, with her Woodswoman Scholarship Fund ensuring that women could continue to get the opportunities they needed. Her writing shows us that the peace and harmony that living in the wild and rubbing up against mother nature can offer isn't just for men, and she brings a spirituality and love with her words that is hard to describe. Perhaps the closest I can get is that what they convey is the sense of a woman living in a constant state of awe.

CHAPTER TEN

It isn't Just Tree Hugging

'Where are you going?'

My little son – fully dressed in his current holiday daywear of pyjamas – was halfway out the front door.

'Out.'

I hadn't expected this till his teenage years.

'Out where?'

'*side.*'

To the sound of the door slamming, I think *Well, that's only a good thing.*

———

It's no secret that I have always been fascinated by nature and biology and have loved being outdoors. I have always known that it is 'good for me' and the kids and everyone. I've come at this from a nostalgic route I think, and I've never really thought too much about it.

The concept of spiritual healing work in nature has never been my bag. Whether it is someone needing a mental break or working through trauma, doing that in the natural world is nothing new though. From shamans guiding ayahuasca ceremonies to Native American healers, many indigenous people knew about the natural world's power to heal humans. Now, we have to make a conscious decision or effort to take our therapy or healing – or just ourselves – outside. On the whole, our default mode is in. In where? *side.*

Now that I am starting to feel the benefits of my own natural world however, I am curious about whether there is science to back it up – and it turns out that there is plenty of new work to study.

Many researchers point to the disconnection between people and the natural world as a contributor to ill health, emotional problems and a lack of psychological well-being. During my training as a coach, I gained a certificate in nature coaching, which 'rests on the very assumption that mother nature holds resources to support the physical, emotional, mental and spiritual well-being for individuals and groups' – the idea, coined by E. O. Wilson in 1984, of biophilia.[1] In the book of the same name, he suggests that humans are emotionally – even subconsciously – connected to wild places because existing outdoors is rooted in our biology and evolution. That makes perfect sense. We evolved from a creature that spent all of its life out in the open. Whether eating, gathering, cooking, drinking, bathing or child-rearing, our ancestors did not spend a single minute of their lives confined within four walls or in front of a screen.

Since I graduated with a degree in ecology and conservation in 1998, phrases like climate change have become terms we use every day. The same is true with our connection to nature: when the environmental movement first began, its roots ran deep, but the idea that we need to feel close to nature wasn't yet in the public consciousness. Since then, things have changed, and for many of us, living through Covid lockdowns fostered an even greater appreciation of that need. This growing consciousness is not just shown in our constant demand for more *Escape to the Country* episodes. It is backed up by science. Whether we like forest bathing, wild swimming, gardening or even just enjoy having plants indoors or a view of something natural from our windows, in recent decades, it's all been studied and research has proven that we feel better when we are surrounded by nature. Research confirms that green spaces increase well-being, energy, vitality and the immune system. They have also been observed to lower levels of stress and fatigue and even relieve headaches and ease respiratory problems. Our bodies did not evolve in this way to live mostly indoors or only exist in urban environments, and there is a huge amount of research into the disconnect between the natural world and the world we actually live in and the adverse effects of that disconnect on our physical, emotional, mental and spiritual well-being.

Shinrin-yoku (Japanese for forest bathing) doesn't mean stripping off and having a bath in the woods; it simply means walking in the woods. I defy you to walk in the woods and not feel good. As humans, we instinctively know this stuff because we know how it makes us feel, but research reveals why. One Japanese study showed that a session of approximately two hours of forest bathing, as part of a day's outing in a forest, led to improvements in physiological health in people of working age.[2] This was illustrated by a decrease in blood pressure and the alleviation of negative psychological parameters. From the same study, what was also significant was that those with depressive tendencies showed a greater improvement in their psychological well-being after one two-hour session of forest bathing compared to those who did not display depressive tendencies.

Phytoncides are the 'essential oils' of trees, and by walking in the woods, we surround ourselves with them. Trees – and other plants – give off these VOCs (volatile organic compounds) to protect themselves. They have anti-microbial and insecticidal, anti-inflammatory, antidepressant and anti-oxidant properties, and so they affect our immune response. There is even evidence to suggest that the Natural Killer (NK) cells we all have, which can kill cancer cells, can increase following a walk in the woods and the results can last for many days.[3] Exposure to these compounds can even reduce blood glucose levels. A lot is going on when we take a walk through the trees, especially if we do some breathing practice at the same time.

Other studies have shown that the parasympathetic and sympathetic nervous systems are affected too. In simple terms, the sympathetic system is the one that springs into gear when the bear walks into your front yard; the parasympathetic system is the one that soothes you afterwards. Walking in the forest has been shown to lower levels of cortisol and increase the activity of the parasympathetic nervous system. It also reduces the activity of the sympathetic nervous system, taking us out of that fight-or-flight state – that in our modern world, we seem to perpetually live in – while helping to enhance our mood. At Stanford University in the US, too, researchers have monitored a measurable reduction in depressive thoughts and negative feelings following a walk in nature, and in the groups they studied, both self-centredness and chronic worrying were reduced.[4]

There are also measurable benefits to visually taking in 'the green scene'. Roger Ulrich, in researching the effects on patients between 1972 and 1981, noticed that being able to see plants and greenery growing from their hospital beds had a positive effect on patients who were recovering from operations: they needed fewer days on painkillers and experienced fewer complications than those patients who were just staring at a wall.[5]

Getting our hands dirty while we are outside is good for us too. In the soil lurk microbes and bacteria, and – far from being a cause for concern and immediate hand-washing – one of them, *Mycobacterium vaccae*, has been shown to boost our levels of serotonin (our brain's feel-good chemical) and norepinephrine (a hormone closely linked to our fight-or-flight response). Dr Christopher Lowry's work at Bristol University showed a positive effect of the bacteria on our mental health and demonstrated that it acted like an antidepressant.[6] He found that after a month of playing in the forest and caring for crops, children in Finland had a healthier diversity of microbes in their guts. Touching the soil, breathing near it or eating traces of the bacteria on our homegrown veg benefits our immune system and mental health and the microbes in our guts.

In 2005, author Richard Louv hit upon the term 'nature-deficit disorder' and described the negative consequences of that disconnect on our children's health in his book *Last Child in the Woods*, starting a whole movement.[7]

These are things I have always known but never really considered. Some inner guide brought me to the countryside, the natural world and gardens as a setting for my life and work that makes me happy and feels 'good' somehow. I have simply taken it for granted that the natural world is a 'good' place to be, but now I find myself re-evaluating. There is no doubting the science here, the proven benefits to mental health and healing, even for trauma. The value to us as individuals of the environment we actually evolved to exist in – the stakes of losing so much wilderness, so much of our natural world, are way higher than I thought.

The chance to feel better lies just outside my door. I grab my wellies and lever my feet into them.

My sleep-ruffled teenage son thumps down the stairs, his limbs now as long as branches.

'Is there anything to eat?'

'Yes, the fridge is full of food.'

'Can you make me something?'

'No, I'm going out.'

'Where?'

'*side*. You should come with me.'

He laughs.

CHAPTER ELEVEN

A Visit to the Zoo

One photo, falling out of a book, brought it all back.

The zoo was deserted, and in the middle of this cloudless African day our parching proximity to the equator could be felt in every silent cell. Not that the place was bursting with cells – quite the opposite, in fact. The bumbling activity of the three of us – me, Liza and the baby chimp swaggering alongside us like a toddler – felt as though we were intruding in a graveyard. There was a reason for that.

A much younger me, in my quest to help with wildlife and conservation in any way, had come to Nigeria to do some volunteer work on a primate conservation project with a little-known primate called the drill. Here, in a walled compound in Calabar, is where I met Liza Gadsby and her husband Peter Jenkins. Liza was the epitome of cool to me. Blonde, skinny, tanned, with a gap between her two front teeth and a 'let's get shit done' energy that just shone out. She was focused and visionary all at the same time and – best of all to me – she knew tons about conservation and actually did it.

The compound contained one small house and many caged enclosures, each one holding drills, chimps or other primates. The house was basic but comfortable, set on one storey with a couple of bedrooms, a tiny kitchen, an office and a big room with sofas and a dining table. Only one room had air conditioning, but it was shady in there and much cooler than outside.

Life was busy, between feeding and caring for the animals, planning the next phase of the conservation programme and dealing with all the people who helped there – PhD students, animal carers, support staff, and my vet friend John Lewis – so there wasn't much time to sit around chatting idly. So I was pleased one morning when Liza invited me on a little outing to the zoo, and even more delighted when she brought along a baby chimp called Pablo. We drove the short distance across town in the Land Rover with Pablo sitting on my lap.

'We drove this here from London,' she told me, 'crossing the Sahara in the summer. Nobody does that – for good reason – and I think we both ended up spending the rest of our lives in south-east Nigeria because our brains were damaged by the heat. We had this little thermometer pasted on our dashboard and by 9am every day it was at 125, which was as high as that thermometer went. By 9am! And on top of that, it was Ramadan so everybody was cranky.

'We grew up in the same town,' Liza said of her husband, Peter. 'We've been together since 1984 or 85, although I knew who he was before then. I had no interest in primates or even the rainforest. I was interested in birds, but we had the option to go on a different type of job when we first got to Nigeria. We were only going to be there for four days on a transit visa – and we are still here, all these years later. Anyway the Nigerian Conservation Foundation, which at that time was doing good work, was looking for volunteers – fools like us – to go to Cross River State and do some survey work about these newly discovered gorillas. They also needed someone to go to the wetlands up in the north in the Sahel, which was a big migratory bird place, and that is what I wanted to do hands down. I wasn't interested in a rainforest or gorillas but Peter wanted to go and we ended up doing what Peter wanted to do . . . I was never driven by drills or rainforest. Anyway that's how we ended up here.'

Today wasn't going to be the delightful kind of zoo visit that it might be in the UK. This zoo had no visitors other than us – it had long been deserted – but it did still have residents, and it was those we had come to see.

'We'll check on the crocs first,' said Liza, 'though I don't have anything to give them today. It's just good to know they are alive at this stage of the game.' Her voice was flat, carrying no optimism, no joy, just a sense that here we were and this was how it was. I had been wildly curious to see a Nigerian zoo for myself, but Liza had met my wide eyes with the glance of someone who had seen all that before and simply said, 'Don't bother to get too excited. Calabar zoo is dead.'

Cracked concrete enclosures stood empty. Channels that might once have carried cool water were dry. Here and there, the odd cluster of plants held on to a faint shade of green but on the whole the colour scheme was brown and beige, the atmosphere heavy and the very air brushing our bare skin with heat.

'It was a zoo that had been built in and remains in the grounds of the state forestry department,' she said as we walked, 'and it was a legacy that went back to the colonial era that every forestry department had to have a zoo or something like that to show off regional animals. There are zoos like that all over Nigeria. All over. Every single one of them awful and animals dying of starvation.

'We went in there just to have a look when we first got here, and we immediately said "this is horrific". There were no other words. No one was properly funding the zoo. Yes, there was money for security – but to protect the property not the animals. There didn't appear to be even the most basic animal care. There was no food, no water. The animals were simply left to die.'

And they did. By the time Liza and Peter had 'negotiated' access from an animal-welfare position, Calabar zoo had already become a tragedy. They discovered mainly skeletons. Occasionally the skeletons still had wisps of life, but in those cases the best thing was to ease the poor souls out of their suffering.

'There was an adult female drill, there was a couple of crocs, a giant python and a female mangabey, and Jacob, a chimp who was about eight or nine years old. We said, "Oh, this is awful. We are never coming back here again."'

But how could they not? And it was Jacob we had really come to see today.

But first the crocs. As we approached a low wall, Pablo the baby chimp held back, slowing then pulling then tugging at Liza's hand, protesting with quiet squats.

'He's been here before,' Liza explained, 'he knows what's in there. And even at his age he knows that he doesn't want to go anywhere near them.'

Liza pulled Pablo up into her arms where he clung so hard around her neck that she didn't need to hold him. He was making such a fuss that Liza stopped a few metres away from the wall.

'Go check they are OK, will ya? I'm not going to put him through it. There should be two of them in there.'

The insects seemed to increase around me as I approached the wall. Uncertain of what I would see or how close the crocs would be, it was with relief that I saw the wall was simply the edge of a deep and very narrow pit. At the bottom was just enough water to make some mud. At first I couldn't see how anything could be alive in there, but after a couple of seconds my eyes tuned in and I could discern the backs, then tails and then protruding crowns of the head and even nostrils of the two long crocs lying side by side.

'I see 'em.'

'Good. OK, OK, in a minute,' said Liza to Pablo, who was panting. 'He wants to go see Jacob.'

'They're just lying side by side in the mud,' I reported.

'Not much else for them to do.'

As I watched, a fly landed on a nostril and a croc head moved lazily to one side. 'One just moved.'

'Well, that's exciting, and about as much as we'll get. They are still alive.'

We crossed a hot sandy space towards some low concrete cubes. I was excited but also nervous to meet Jacob. I tried to remember all the rules: don't look him directly in the eye; allow him to come to you; don't put your hand in; remember he is way stronger than you – an adult chimp can pull your arm off. I had butterflies in my stomach, but they were a mere appetiser for the gut punch.

Pablo, in the way of baby chimps, swung himself off Liza and onto the floor, speeding ahead of us on front knuckles and back legs, hooting out a greeting. He was headed towards a concrete box that bounced back the glare of the sun so brightly that at first it was hard to see much else. I gradually made out thick iron bars. A huff came from the darkness inside and then something I have never forgotten, perhaps because I took a photo at that moment: from between the bars, a large, pale chimpanzee hand reached out and the fingers tenderly met Pablo's tiny ones.

I stepped onto the wide concrete sill that fronted the cage, and I could finally see him. Jacob, a fully grown, yet slight, male chimpanzee, trapped in a cell of bars around ten by ten feet. Even the floor was made of bars, and all that was encased in a cell of concrete, a cell that he would spend eleven years of his life in.

The first thing I did was look in his eyes. It was instinctive, though it didn't matter as he wasn't paying me the slightest attention. His black eyes were transfixed by the toddler we had brought to see him, and already they were playing hand-chase games through the bars.

We stood silently for a while, watching. It gave me a chance to take it all in: the squalor, the absence of absolutely anything of any interest in his barred box, the heat, his isolation, the sheer cruelty, the size and smell of Jacob yet his complete tenderness with baby Pablo. Like I said, a gut punch.

'Hey fella,' Liza's tone was soft as she crouched beside the bars and opened her bag, 'how ya doin' today?' She pulled out a bottle of cool water and unscrewed the lid. 'We brought you some water and some food, here.'

She held the bottle through the bars but looked at the ground in front of her. Gently, he took it and raised it to his

mouth, pursing his lips. I couldn't imagine how thirsty he
must be, and yet he paused. Pablo was begging for the
water. He certainly didn't need it – all the orphaned chimps
in Liza and Peter's care had as much water as they needed
on hand all the time, and plenty of food too – but Pablo
wanted this water. And Jacob, who must have been so
thirsty, before drinking a drop pushed the bottle through
the bars and into Pablo's outreached hands. The young
chimp immediately began to pour it out, then when Liza
tried to grab the precious water from him, he ran away
laughing in that grimacing way that chimps have, stopping
to turn back and see our reaction while he continued to
play with the water.

'No matter,' said Liza, who was obviously prepared and
knew the drill because she drew another full water bottle
from her bag. 'The truth is – and this is why we always try to
bring a chimp with us – of all the things he yearns for while
he is here, social interaction is the most important. Boys
come from the town sometimes to torture him – that is
how he got that wound beside his eye. When Peter found
him they were trying to poke his eye out with a stick, yet he
thought it was a game. He was so desperate for any kind of
interaction that he would even be bullied.'

In bed that night – and in the many years that followed
– I couldn't help but think of Jacob. Of his loneliness. I
returned on numerous occasions during my trip and one
time, while leaning against the bars, felt Jacob's fingers on
my arm and realised he was grooming me. 'Your turn, it's
rude not to,' I was told. So I parted the thick hairs on his
arm, peering down to the pale skin and pretending to pluck
out insects. These interactions were as important, if not
more so, than the water, fulfilling a deep-seated need that
even thirst could wait for. A need for company. The plan was
to incorporate Jacob into the conservation programme for
the drills and the long-term rescue programme for the
chimpanzees.

'Jacob was like a skeleton,' Liza said when I asked what he was like when they first found him. 'He was just like the way you see the images of people when they freed Auschwitz – hairless, skin and bones. At that time we had Pansy, our first chimpanzee, and she was a tiny little thing, maybe a year old. She was just clinging to Peter, this spoiled little baby who had all the care in the world. After we realised the others were dead, we saw Jacob and we thought, "OMG, look at that chimp, we have to do something for this poor chimp." So we turned around and went outside and found a woman in the street selling big beautiful papaya. We went back and the papaya didn't fit through the bars, so Peter took out his pocket knife and slit it in half lengthwise and passed it through the bars to Jacob. We were sitting nose to nose on either side of the bars – Jacob and Peter and me – and Peter was holding Pansy. Jacob took this papaya and he didn't just stuff it into his mouth, he just held it and looked at it as if he was thinking, "This is a thing of beauty." He was a very unusual male. And at that moment, pampered, spoiled Pansy reached out her little hand to him with the begging gesture and went,' Liza pursed her lips in perfect mimicry of a chimp face and uttered super-gentle *ohh*s just like a begging chimp does, 'and Jacob broke off over half the papaya and pushed it out through the bars to her. We both looked at each other and said, "We have to take care of this animal for the rest of his life."

'His strategy was to engage you. When you gave him his food, he would take it and he sorted it. He had everything stashed: OK, cucumbers over here and papaya over here, green vegetables here . . . He would have everything neatly stacked and then he would say OK, now it's time to play and he did whatever he could to keep you there for as long as possible because the social contact was more important to him.'

I was in awe of Liza. She wasn't like any other woman I had ever met and she redefined what being a woman looked like to me. Normally it was men out there doing shit, but here was Liza – doing her own shit and owning a really quite challenging life. She took everything – and I mean literally everything – in her stride, looked good doing it, frankly, and grinned a lot. We spayed a neighbour's cat on her kitchen table in exchange for a bucket of prawns for dinner. She had hired a chef named Fantastic to help feed the growing team of volunteers and, when he turned out to be anything but fantastic, I heard her every day patiently teaching him the basics, like how to crack an egg. When the youngest of the chimpanzee tribe came inside for his bottle and stole her husband's very expensive fountain pen, Liza was the picture of calm, pausing her discussion on a medical evaluation of a male drill and sipping her drink while her husband chased the little chimp around and around the coffee table and chaos ensued. Every time something was needed she was there. Every time it thundered, for example, someone had to go and sit with the terrified baby chimps, and so I found myself led by Liza into their enclosure to simply sit on the floor in the torrential rain and be clambered upon and hugged by twelve baby chimps. And those were just her side gigs. In fact, so was Jacob. The real reason for her being in Nigeria was the conservation of a primate – not the chimp but the drill.

In the Calabar compound, drills were all around us. Although I had never seen one before and had to confess to not having heard about them before, I had rapidly become very familiar with them. They were the talk of the dinner table, the breakfast table and pretty much everything in between. Imagine a baboon and you would be pretty close to a drill. Indeed, along with mandrills, they were identified as part of the same family as baboons until relatively recently but now sit in a group of their own. The drill is grey with a long face. The males can sport a lot of colour – a red on the behind or surrounding their genitals, just to remind the females how spectacular they are or maybe to give them a clue where to look – while female colouration is plain and simple, and the females are smaller.

Together, Peter and Liza had started a much-needed captive breeding and reintroduction project as part of a long-term conservation strategy for this species in desperate need. In the 1980s, they found themselves traipsing around the jungle, surveying for drills in their native habitat in Nigeria and Cameroon. Drill numbers had become dangerously low because of habitat loss and enthusiastic hunting – so low that through the 1980s they were assumed to be extinct in most of their range. Although humans are familiar with primates, particularly the chimpanzee, drills didn't really have a high profile. They didn't do or breed particularly well in zoos so they didn't have the same 'exposure' as some of the other animals in dire need of protecting, which also meant they were overlooked by much of the conservation community.

The good news was the discovery that scant populations did still exist in the wild, and so the International Union for Conservation of Nature put them on the endangered list and they became better known. Those populations were really fragmented, though, which severely impacted the natural movement of mating individuals between groups. It is this kind of movement that maximises the gene pool and keeps the individuals healthy. Fragmentation leads to small isolated populations and in-breeding and all the problems that come with it.

At that stage, little was known about the drill, their ecology, biology or where to find them in the wild, so I suppose it was no surprise that even I – with my passion for wildlife – hadn't ever heard of them. Yet here I was, surrounded by them.

I have so many incredible memories from my time with the project, including the long drive I took with Peter and Liza to the Afi River Forest Reserve. There we went to a remote village, where my white skin made me a complete novelty but we talked and engaged and brought gifts and were welcomed. Peter and Liza were working with the village elders to see if they could come up with a mutually beneficial plan to safeguard an area of the forest for the drills and for the conservation work to continue. It would also mean that hunting for drills would have to stop, which would be a challenge but the conversations were underway.

The conditions and terrain were tough and I was amazed at the ambition of it. One idea was to fence a huge area of the forest to keep the primates protected. Standing in the middle of the forest and looking at the dense undergrowth, I wondered if that could ever be achieved. But that was all in the future and my time here had run out – I had to get back to my day job and a different kind of real world in 90s London.

CHAPTER TWELVE

Decades On

With reliable internet and less of a hectic schedule, lockdown meant I could eventually catch up with Liza. During Covid, she and Peter had had no choice but to return from Nigeria to the States as Peter had been ill and needed medical attention and time to recuperate. After all these years, I asked Liza what happened to Jacob.

'He made it up to Afi,' she told me. It took many years after my visit, but they had finally protected the forest I visited and it was now the Afi Mountain Wildlife Sanctuary; their plans to provide a home for primates there had materialised. When they got him out of the zoo, their dream for Jacob had come true and they had been able to take him there, 'but he was so much older than our other chimpanzees so we had to build a secure handling structure just for him. So we did that, and we transported him up there and we moved him into that. The other chimps were in an electrified enclosure but we didn't think Jacob could go in there because he didn't have nearly enough socialising experience and we didn't think it would be secure enough for him. We were pretty sure that meeting all these other chimps in that kind of way would be traumatic for him, so he stayed in the handling facility for ten years. Finally we built the new enclosure for the chimps, which was like twenty-five acres (which is why it took so long), and that was completed in 2010. It was absolutely massive – we are talking twelve hectares or so. Then we started the process of moving the chimps from the old enclosure into this big new one.

'All this time, we would bring individuals in to make friends with Jacob in his own enclosure and he was always the boss, in the nicest possible way, and he tolerated a lot from the other chimps and he was always incredible. You know what he was like. Anyway, finally we were ready to try to integrate him into the new enclosure in the forest.

I wasn't there, and Jacob went out and the other adult males were intimidating, and I think we made a mistake . . . He was in there for a couple of weeks, to make a long story short, and they killed him. They murdered him.'

I had no idea what to say in response. We were both silent.

'It must have been a huge loss.' Liza's face said it all. 'After all that time.'

'I know,' she said, 'but we had to come to terms with it. He enjoyed his life even though he was still in a cage up there because he had constant attention and he had friends and good food and he had cage mates sometimes and relationships and he was always happy. I mean, he always loved women, and you could still go to him when you had a splinter in your finger and he would get it out. He was the only chimp – male or female – that I ever really completely trusted.'

I think back to what his life had been in the zoo, and how Peter and Liza had first saved it and then slowly transformed it, and of course she is right. But it's still such a shock to think that ultimately his death came because of other chimps.

'Adult male chimps. Chimps are like humans,' she said, 'they are the only other species that murders their own kind for no other reason than perhaps they are assholes. And of course it's mostly the men. But they are also the only other species that laughs out loud. They're not animals and they're not humans. Working with chimps, it's like ET, it's like something from another planet, a whole other creature. Chimpanzees are really something else.'

We are 98.8 per cent similar, and somewhere in that 98.8 is the dark side, but I'm intrigued by her nod to the difference between male and female chimps.

'There are lots of differences. From working with primates, I have learned and come to believe it's just there. As a parent, I'm sure you've spent time reading about the whole nature v nurture thing. There was a phase in women's rights where the thought was that girls only act like girls because they are given dolls to play with instead of guns. Well, there may be something to that but I've actually come to believe it's much more nature; we females are so different from the get-go, from birth.

'We treat male and female primates exactly the same but they are fundamentally different in their strategies to life. There is a biological basis for that. The whole biological imperative of every living creature is to reproduce, but for most mammal species, most male vertebrates, all they have to do is a few minutes' investment in fertilising eggs. That's it. Whereas a female has to have access to resources, security, she needs to have social skills if she is living in a social species like primates or many other animals, she needs to have friends and support . . . She has to have those things. Males don't have to, they can be assholes, they can be loners. All they have to do is come in and pass on their sperm successfully and they have fulfilled their mission in life.

'If you give a two- or three- or ten- or twenty-year-old female chimpanzee a bucket of water, she is going to sit down and put her arms around it and secure it. First of all she's going to look around and see "OK, who's going to come and mess with my bucket of water?" and then she's going to figure out what to do with it. She might drink some, she might make a leaf sponge, or if she has a cloth she's going to wash that rag, herself, her hands, her feet. She sees it as a resource to be conserved and used. A male chimp, if you give him a bucket of water, he's going to pick it up, he doesn't mind about the water, he'll spill the water, and use the bucket as a weapon or a toy and throw it at somebody.

'Women naturally have to conserve resources to achieve their biological imperative, which is passing on their genes. It's a long-term investment. Conservation is a long-term investment, and the problem with much conservation that I have witnessed in West Africa is that conservation

programmes are too short-term – one or two or three years
aren't going to do anything. If you want to compare it to
men and women, it's short-term investment,' she laughed.
'Long-term investment is a different attitude. Women have
more staying power, and I'm not saying it's because we are
better creatures or any of that; it's just our biological
imperative, right? Maybe women see that relationships
matter, that long-term investment of time, resources and
your caring, all those things are critical to success. It's
generational. And any conservation initiative, in order to
succeed, has to be generational.'

We shared some memories of my visit, particularly an
attempt we made to put two male drills in a large enclosure.
They had never met.

'We were in the early learning stage,' Liza said, 'and
nobody knew much about drills – there were no drill
experts, zoos had not succeeded in breeding drills, nobody
had successfully managed a group of drills in captivity – and
we were now the victims of our own success. We had too
many captive drills but nobody knew how to do this. Drills
and mandrills for some reason were never kept in large
groups in captivity, but we needed to and we were trying to
prove that it could be done. We have certainly proved that
many times over now, but at the time it was all a learning
experience. Now we know more and that, yes, drills do live
in multiple-male groups. But with any enclosure, if they
wanna escape they can.'

That was the situation we faced one day as we all prepared
for the 'meet-up' of the two males. All the talk the night
before was about whether the enclosure was big enough for
them to take some space away from each other, whether
there were enough different areas, foliage and whether the
fence was high enough.

'You know what we learned? That it's not a question of
whether the enclosure's not good enough. You have to make
it so they don't want to escape, that it's nice enough to be

inside, that it's the place to be because of the society, because of the food. If they feel they need to escape they will. That is something we didn't know then.'

What we worried about more than anything else was that they were going to get into some terrible fight and John the vet was going to have to stitch them up. That turned out not to be the problem at all. What shocked us all was that, within minutes of being introduced to the enclosure, the younger of the two drills simply flew over the fence. How he did it none of us saw because it was just so fast and the fence was at least twenty feet high. But do it he did, and we could track his progress because from the other side of the wall came a lot of screaming as he interrupted people going about their day. Suddenly all thoughts turned to what damage he could do to himself or to the people of Calabar in his anxious state, and every vehicle from moped to Land Rover was immediately pressed into action. After a long while, sleeping off a tranquilliser dart, he was rescued before any damage was done. We immediately took him to the air-conditioned office because their thermoregulatory system doesn't work as well when they are tranquillised and he had just been exerting himself in the midday sun. Thankfully he woke none the worse for wear and was returned to his previous enclosure. It was just another step along the way to learning how to conserve this little known species. Over the years, Peter and Liza discovered that, in general, big males will stay in an enclosure because that's where the females are, and the females stay in because that is where their children are. So, who escapes? Low ranking males and childless females.

'Over the years, we have seen some terrible fights and some terrible injuries,' said Liza, 'but really these males are much too proud of their spectacular appearance and they really don't want to get injured. They will avoid it at all costs.'

Presumably that spectacular appearance is helpful in passing on the genes?

'Well, I think so but there's been published papers to say that the adult male drills have these wonderful colours and it's the male with the brightest colours that becomes the dominant male and attracts the female. I think that's absolute rubbish. Some of the brightest males I've seen have been males that aren't even with a group. We had one male who was completely crippled from the waist down and he kind of lived free range and could do whatever he wanted to, and he became the most colourful male – in terms of those classic drill colours in the groin and the rump and the face – of any male we have ever had, and he couldn't have even mounted a female if he had the opportunity.'

'So I wonder what it is, then?'

'The females choose who the dominant male is – and this is where it is really interesting in terms of how females affect the future. The males can fight and some guy can appoint himself, or the other males can even respect him, but if the females don't support him he's not going to be the dominant male because sex is by choice. The females choose to have sex with you – they allow you to have sex with them and it's not forced – and so if the females don't want you, you are not going to be *the* guy. And the guys that they like are those that pay attention to them every day of the month, not only the week when they are in oestrus, when their swelling is up. The females like the guys that are nice to their children. They like the guys that keep peace in the group. That's what they value the most. They want a safe environment for their families, for their children. The smart high-ranking females often avoid fights and support the quietest most peaceful males because they know what is needed for them to successfully pass their genes on, which is to have a safe environment. They don't give a shit how colourful the male is, they want him to do his goddam job. I find it rather amusing that people assume that the biggest and most colourful or the best fighter is going to be the dominant male.'

'Do drill females live much beyond their reproductive age?' I asked Liza. 'Do they have a menopause?'

'No, and this is something we have been able to observe. Females live a lot longer than males, and I think there is a variety of reasons for that, but they never stop cycling and during the week that they are ovulating they get this big swelling. Fortunately we don't, chimpanzees get it, gorillas don't get it. There have been some credible theories to say that it's tied to the type of social system that the species has. When you have multiple males in a group, the dominant male needs to be able to make sure he can spread his genes. He needs to have a signal when the female is ovulating and he needs to get to her. You take a species like gorillas – where they just have single-male groups, polygynous groups – and he doesn't need that.

'It all kind of relates to your main theme here,' Liza continued, 'and that is assumptions about females, motivations and biology. We evolved in the wild the same as men, and we are more durable. Like female drills, we live longer than men on the whole. I'm a real sort of anti-feminist, I can't stand people talking about "the first woman this" and "the first woman that". It reduces somebody's achievements because it's sort of like "oh, it's great *for a woman*" or "you're only being recognised because you're female", and I resent it. There is this thing in the last ten or twenty years where girls are not supposed to be good at maths or science. I don't get it. "Oh, I'm just a girl, I can't do science." When did that start? I remember in school the girls were much better at maths than the boys and in fact better academically on the whole. It's something created by modern media. I never felt that there was any insinuation or discouragement that because I was a girl I couldn't do that. I'm sixty-three and I see this now and it seems more recent than in my education. It's very damaging and it's so embedded in the culture and in advertising that we actually have to address it.'

'One of the things that I think is a bigger driving force,' I said, 'is passion. It doesn't matter what the obstacles are if the love is there. Where did that passion come from for you?'

'In terms of animals and the outdoors, that had always been a passion since I was a child, but my major in university was biology, and it started with my real interest and love being for birds, not primates, not even mammals. That all started in high school, I think.

'I'm not in the wilderness very much anymore, I don't get to be. I don't like the expression "sustainable development" because it doesn't exist, but "sustainable protection" should be the goal of everyone in conservation, and you're not going to achieve that by having a good time wandering around in the bush. You may discover some interesting things but you're not protecting anything, you're indulging yourself to a large degree. If you want to achieve something for these places, you need to be out of them, talking with people, talking with government, trying to raise awareness and support and interest for these places or these species. For those people who say "I just love the wilderness and I just have to be there, it's my soul, it's when I feel alive," that's fine, but that is all about you. Great! But don't act like you're the great saviour of these places. The same with a lot of research that goes on today: you're just collecting a bunch of data so that you can take it home and get your PhD. If it doesn't have any useful application? Fine, but don't parade yourself as a great conservationist just because you are filling in the blanks for your career.

'It doesn't matter about me seeing these things or even experiencing them; I just want to know that they are there and they are safe. That's much more important and that is what motivates me. Sure, I'd love to spend more time in the wilderness and that's partly what motivates me. We have to have the wilderness, right? Any biologist or anybody who reads the newspaper should understand today that we have to have it for this planet to survive and that we don't have enough of it. We have very little and we are still losing it. Come on, people, when are we going to wake up?'

'But we evolved to be "out there", didn't we?'

'Yes, but with our freaking phones on all the time, we forget to be there completely. When you are in a true wilderness place there's an element of danger and you are on alert and you are completely in it, but more and more in our modern lives we are distracted. When you are out there in the true wilderness you are completely in situ, in the moment, in reality and there is something very healthy for our minds about that. That's who we were – all senses on high alert, your sense of smell, your sense of cold or warm, your hearing, your eyesight, everything. You are using it all and that is how we evolved and that's how other creatures live.'

We returned to talking about the drill project and the future. Liza was less than optimistic. Covid affected primates as well as humans, and things up in Afi River have changed. The camp was on the receiving end of some crime and violence, which destroyed some of the trust and relationships that had been built over the last decades. After a spell in Washington State, Liza was keen to get back, but not so sure about what would happen next.

'What we achieved since the beginning was possible because of terrific support from state (and federal) government, starting with the military government for our first five years, followed by two successive state (and federal) civilian administrations who supported what we and others were doing for conservation – the creation of protected areas, etc. This ended in 2015, when we had a state administration come in that did not support conservation or protection of state areas and pulled all support for us and for relevant state agencies. It's been heartbreaking to watch the work of so many over decades unravel. What holds a country like

Nigeria together is traditional culture. A big part of that is respect for the elders and in places that has gone.

'And there's climate change. It's very discouraging for anyone working in our field. You feel like, "Well, I just wasted my whole life – it's all a goner." What has to happen for people to believe it?'

CHAPTER THIRTEEN

Looking Back Again

I have always been led to believe that, as a woman, even though I can have equal rights and opportunities, it should somehow be in my nature to be nurturing, to be sensible and responsible, that somehow those things are hardwired in me and also that is my duty to perform them. Yet men don't have to be that way. They are the 'providers', the 'hunters'; it is their job to be manly and go out into the world and face demons and have adventures.

We all have this hangover from the historic idea that we evolved from a hunter-and-gatherer society where the gender roles were really specific. But why then do I need adventure? Why do I need every day to be different and challenging? Why do I have such an urge to go out into the world if my place is here by the fire with the kids and a wooden spoon? Why is it not enough to just load the dishwasher every day? Why am I bored by the very concept of the domestic goddess?

I get the nurturing part. As someone who wasn't that bothered about having children in the first place, the natural way my heart fell deeply in love and my instincts to care for and understand these little humans took me by surprise, and I'm always happiest when we are all together – that bond is very real. But how have our perceptions of our role been so skewed?

There is no doubt that much of our history was written about men by men. It is unfortunate but true that the education of women was hardly prioritised until relatively recent times, keeping them out of the debate, their voices hushed, their passions even more so. A passionate woman was considered perhaps out of control, dangerous, certainly not one who fit the place society had destined her for. Only comparatively recently are we truly coming out of that ridiculous fog and, as we do, ideas about our evolutionary history are changing too.

The first fossil hunter to find a complete skeleton of an ichthyosaur, a plesiosaur and a pterosaur – Mary Anning – wasn't even allowed to vote or attend meetings at the Geological Society of London because she had a pair of boobs.

———

'Lucy' is probably the best-known female fossil. She was discovered in Ethiopia in 1974 and was named after the Beatles song that was playing as the archaeologists celebrated her discovery with beers under the African skies. The book about her (another that has been on my shelf since my late teens) was described as a 'controversial bestseller', the controversy being due to the fact that she provided clear evidence that bipedalism developed long before large skull size. Hers was the first skeleton to prove that, in the definition of what made us human, having brains big enough to create language and tools actually came after the ability to consistently walk upright. Until then, the theory had been that the brains came first. Lucy's skull, jaws and teeth (and examples of others found nearby) had a primitive ape-like structure that was to identify her as a hominid new to science – *Australopithecus afarensis*. Yet it was the 'why' that really caused all the fuss, because it meant that all the scientists had to have a little rethink. It had been assumed that humans went bipedal to leave their hands free to use tools, but this new small-brained reality meant these bipedal hominids were clearly not developed enough to be using tools yet. That theory was already pretty much out of the window. Another theory – that early hominids went bipedal to see further afield because they had moved out of the forest and were now living on the plains – was, frankly, a bit iffy to start with and now it was decidedly more so.

Instead, the theory of why our 'ancestors' made this monumental move to stand upright and walk on two legs was possibly, according to Owen Lovejoy (the locomotion expert in chapter sixteen of *Lucy*), to do with sex. (I just want to make it clear: this is nothing to do with the ability to have sex standing up.) Specifically, Lovejoy was theorising that walking on two legs was part of a strategy to enable our ancestors to reproduce more quickly. (Again, this has nothing to do with the speed of standing-up sex.)[1]

Bipedalism wasn't really of benefit for speed, though – the old two-legged gait isn't that energy efficient either, particularly when it comes to running – so why did our ancestors bother with it? What advantage did it bring? Lovejoy suggests it was all linked to our reproductive strategy. Walking upright, and in a secure committed relationship (yes, seriously), early man hominid would happily go off for the day, leaving early woman hominid at home with the little ones. Then, because his hands were free, he was able to carry meat home for them. Since the food was being brought to her, the female was able to have more children and, after another few millennia or so, they didn't even need to cling to her because she had no need to travel long distances or hunt for herself, so that was probably when the grasping feet dropped off the evolutionary radar. The female was now free to lactate and gestate as much as was possible while being provisioned. (I am somewhat crudely summarising.)

In his paper 'The Origin of Man',[2] Lovejoy refers to the fact that advanced primates typically have a long period where the infant is completely dependent upon the adult. Chimps, for example, according to Jane Goodall, generally stay with their mothers until they are five or six. We also see this in other advanced mammals. While the mother is so taken up with her infant, she doesn't tend to reproduce, so population growth is limited. On top of that, a female chimp doesn't even start reproducing till she is about ten years old.

Lovejoy says that 'strong social bonds, higher levels of intelligence, intense parenting and long periods of learning' all found in higher primates like chimps increase the likelihood of a long life and of survival against external influences like predators, but they don't increase the rate of reproduction. He argues that any species that could reduce the space of time between births would be able to increase the population growth rate, and he uses equations to justify this. I have no intention of repeating such language here.

Yet this is interesting stuff because it all hinges on the females. Bear in mind that, at this stage of the evolution game, our hominid has not yet got a massive brain so they don't yet have complex tool use, or social systems or dishwashers, vodka martinis, leg warmers or even a parish council. All they have is the ability to walk upright.

Females physically carried their babies, which would understandably diminish a female's feeding range, whereas males could roam further and explore different feeding areas. Staying in one place could mean that females were more familiar with the resources and shelters there, would reduce their exposure to predators or accidents in unfamiliar terrain and allow 'intensification of parenting behaviour'. (I can only assume that here Lovejoy means the ability to do more jigsaws, join more pre-verbal music groups or indulge in more complex cupcake-making sessions.)

All those things alone could theoretically help survival. However, if the male and female are monogamous and pair-bonded for life then another interesting thing happens. First of all, the male doesn't need to worry about a loss of 'consort opportunity' – that is to say, someone swooping in on his missus and implanting their genes while he is off collecting meat with his newly available hands. Secondly, he would be pretty much guaranteed that when he brought the food back he would be investing his energy in his own biological unit and the continuation of his own genes.

So it happened, according to Lovejoy's theory, that an advantageous strategy came into being: the males would provision the females, bringing them food while they stayed put. And more calories presumably enabled them to give birth more and lactate more. Furthermore, if the male were then to start 'provisioning' the older infants too, the female – safe in the knowledge that they were fed – could have even more babies, and the male would thereby be increasing his reproductive success even more.

This involvement by males in the process of parenting, suggests Lovejoy, is possibly the only way that Miocene hominids could create any significant increase in their reproductive rate. If we look around for examples, he says, we find it is only among primates whose males directly related themselves in parenting in this way that we find monogamy.

I find this interesting: not only are we seeing the massive step forward of bipedalism, but potentially we are seeing, for women, the start of incarceration and it was pre-human. Sorry, rather than incarceration I mean the seeds of some kind of romantic love, aka monogamy. It's not too much of a push, after all: many animals and birds pair-bond for life or at least have long-term relationships, and it benefits the group.

I have heard arguments to say that men are more likely to sleep around or have affairs because that is how they are dictated to by their genes. In fact, pre-human history could indicate that their genes are telling them completely the opposite.

Here's the other thing: the female *Australopithecus* seems, ultimately, to have the upper hand. None of us females wanders round with a sign – biological or literal – to say we are 'in season', 'receptive', 'ovulating' or that 'implantation is possible at any moment'. It's a cunning evolutionary move by female genes called 'concealed ovulation' that basically means vying males haven't got a clue. From a 'when to attempt to mate' perspective, it's all a bit hit and miss. For all that the males know, some other male could be trying the hit-and-miss tactic on the same sexy *sapiens* they are trying to claim. We females can get pregnant at any time, so if a man wants exclusivity he had better be sure to stay close and attentive. These factors, says Lovejoy, 'would require copulatory vigilance' in both the male and the female if they are to ensure reproductive success. Copulatory vigilance, eh? Sounds sexy.

Being bipedal didn't come with the same birthing problems as we have now. Lucy's offspring would have had a small cranium – no larger than a chimp's – so giving birth multiple times without the assistance of surgical procedures would have been more straightforward, at least until babies with bigger craniums evolved in the *Homo* genus.

Lovejoy also points out that, whereas in other primate groups a family of offspring revolves around the mother, perhaps in early hominid groups like Lucy's – where a pair bond led not only to paternity but also to paternal investment – a family might revolve around both parents rather than just one. That could increase both the birth and survival rates of the offspring.

His argument that a primitive nuclear family, rather than maternal culture, could be the human base of evolution is convincing and, I have to say, heartening somehow. The idea that family bonds and relationships and even sexual monogamy were precursors – motivators for brain and tool development, the origin of home, the basis of us since the dawn of the Pleistocene – fills me with hope. If Owen Lovejoy's theory is true, it is the greatest love story of all time.

CHAPTER FOURTEEN

A Rewrite?

Hold on a minute. I just got completely sucked into it, didn't I? Talk about a little oxytocin leak. Have I just fallen into the 'historic science written by males and the way they want to see things' trap? Well, it appears I am not the only person becoming more acutely aware of this phenomenon. Far from it.

With Lucy, science had taken a step forward: it wasn't because early hominids were smart that they became bipedal; it was because they were bipedal that they were able to become smart. OK, great, but that was nothing specifically to do with the female of the species. Some of the resulting spin-off theories gave me a possible insight into female prehistory, but surely there had to be more than that?

This isn't easy stuff to research. I type into Google 'fossil record women' and I get 'do you mean fossil record human?' NO, I DON'T. Part of the problem is that sexual behaviour, gender roles and the origins of what we women were or weren't doing leave very little in the way of fossils. Partner that now with the way our history seems to show women: as the products of the paradigm of the way men have wanted to see things.

It was Friedrich Nietzsche who said, 'All things are subject to interpretation. Whichever interpretation prevails at a given time is a function of power and not truth.' Well, we find ourselves – without throwing any mud at male scientists – in a sticky situation and it's still tricky to unearth some solid facts about what we women are or aren't really evolved or programmed to do. Yes, as a woman, some of my motivators are clear: protecting and nurturing my children, community, friends, shelter, warmth, love, long-term commitment (to echo Liza). Yet some are not – some of the urges are for a life with a little more adrenaline, dopamine, wilderness, whatever it is. So how do you explain that? We have a whole slew of new scientific techniques at our disposal, and my curiosity about the original wild woman is only growing.

It turns out I'm not alone in my wonderings. Nor am I crazy. According to Athena Aktipis, 'The study of human evolution has tended to look at things from a male perspective, and even adaptations specific to females – like their social behavior and concealed ovulation – have been viewed in terms of how males shape them.'[1]

Athena is associate professor of psychology at Arizona State University and senior author of a paper published in 2021 that challenges the long-held ideas about why concealed ovulation may have evolved. I am thrilled to have been able to track her down and curious to talk it through on a call; I'd have been even more thrilled to visit her, as the sun is always shining in Arizona where she is based.

Her paper proposes that the development of concealed ovulation, as opposed to the very obvious signals and swellings that often indicate ovulation in primates like drills, may not have all been driven by men. Perhaps, Athena suggests, the benefit was to be found in concealing ovulation from other women instead. This premise is called the 'female rivalry hypothesis' because perhaps the female population contained an element of competition as well as co-operation, and concealed ovulation provided some benefit in relation to that.

Using computer-based models with 'agents' (individuals that could be programmed to act in different ways), the team were able to run models of different behaviour patterns over many generations. First they used a model where females could be aggressive with one another. In this they used promiscuous males and non-promiscuous males, the promiscuous ones being the least likely to lend a hand with the child-rearing or share their resources.

Next they used a model where there was no female-to-female aggression programmed in. So when was there any benefit to concealed ovulation? When did they have more children and get commitment from males to share the work?

When females with concealed ovulation were programmed with female-to female-aggression, concealed ovulation had a benefit, these females were actually more successful because they were able to avoid aggression from other females. The females who conceal ovulation do better than those who don't when there is aggression, and they had more children and more commitment from males to share the work.

OK, so it's a computer model and these aren't real humans, but it offers a different and valid insight and at minimum a different paradigm. But why?

'Female sociality and other adaptations are not just about securing male investment, even though that has long been the underlying assumption about the purpose of female social behaviour,' said Athena. 'For a very long time in the evolutionary behaviour world (which is all the more complex because it is multi-disciplinary), there was this idea that males competed and women choose the best of the males. Maybe, for the male scientists, that's what it felt like but it shows a neglect of the interpersonal processes that are happening between females. So, if there was female rivalry, say for a mate, concealed ovulation would benefit an individual female by allowing them to avoid aggression or competition from other females. This wasn't really considered previously.'[2]

I guess it's a good way of keeping the peace.

'Another, good example of the kind of thinking that we've always had is what seems to have been a blind spot in evolutionary psychology and evolutionary anthropology, which is to see or think about the psychological mechanisms that women have for surviving childbirth. It is a critical moment in time for reproductive success and survival. Your survival and your baby's survival in labour and during birth, at this one point of time makes all the difference. The selection pressures at that very moment are crazy strong, right? So this is an area that we need to study more. It is likely that women would possibly have done this together, supporting the woman in labour, sharing wisdom from other births but from a functional evolutionary perspective we just don't know enough about the "systems" that were in place among females for dealing with that. There is a lot of room for study here, and again it is one place where that male-oriented paradigm has neglected a whole really significant topic.'[3]

I'm intrigued by the idea of female-to-female aggression, whether it really existed or not, and what it looked like. Since females were not 'supposed' to be aggressive – because that isn't how we like to think of women – was it simply too uncomfortable a thought for those scientists and therefore it didn't really occur to them? I mean, it's an uncomfortable thought for me; I always rely on women for a sense of community, not to be my rivals. Also in the back of my mind lurks the fact that canine teeth in females post-Lucy slowly showed a reduction in size, implying a reduction in the need for any kind of aggressive behaviour, which suggests a lesser need for fighting or even snarling and bluffing. Was it only the males doing all that now?

'There is evidence for aggression in our fossil record,' Athena says, 'but then it becomes difficult to know who was the aggressor. We can see evidence of cuts and bruises on bones, but it's likely that for females it wasn't necessarily actual physical aggression. Far more likely is that it was an increase in personal, verbal and indirect aggression. That is less costly physically and as a female your physicality and your health has more impact on your ability to reproduce, to become pregnant, to go through labour, so physical aggression would be a last resort. The hope is that we inspire much more consideration of female interactions when we are looking for insights.'

Of course, nothing is simple when it comes to humans anyway. Athena – deeply passionate about her science – is keen to explain more.

'Humans haven't got one specific mating system either,' she tells me. 'Humans are flexible and respond to the conditions, whether they are social, ecological or environmental. Our mating psychology is really interesting: we do show monogamy in same-sex and heterosexual relationships but also polygyny (where there is one male and multiple females), polygynandry (where there are multiple males and females), and polyandry (where there is one female and multiple males).'

'So,' I ask, drawing her back to my original thought, 'how much has the male paradigm really affected our view of the female role in history? Are we getting worked up over nothing?'

'If you look at contemporary hunter-gatherers – and I have spent time with the Hadza people in Tanzania and other groups – what you see is women digging for tubers, foraging, water-collecting, talking, socialising all the while, often with babies on their back or accompanied by young children. If you look at the actual energetics, it is the women's work that enables the community. Rather than calories from hunting, it is the foraging calories that women are mostly gathering that actually sustains life. Hunting adds valuable protein and the results can occasionally be significant, but the results and success rates really vary – a big animal here and there, but more often smaller animals – and a hunting expedition is energetically expensive to the group. So it is probably not the case, after all, that the hunters were actually supporting the group. That being said, humans have different subsistence systems, not just hunter-gatherers but also pastoral systems where the dynamics are different again. Then, once you start a system where wealth is accumulated and you can pass that on to the next generation, then males become much more concerned with paternity.'

Wow, I wasn't expecting the role of men to become quite so insignificant in my mind.

Leaving Athena to the Arizona sunshine, I begin to peruse *Lady Sapiens*, a recent book by Thomas Cirotteau, Jennifer Kerner, Eric Pincas and Philippa Hurd, that promises a less paternal slant on our 'herstory'.[4] It seeks to tell a true and evidence-based story of the kind of woman who might be living in the Upper Palaeolithic. Lucy lived 3.9 to 2.55 million years ago, whereas *Lady Sapiens* attempts to understand a more modern woman who lived during the period between 40,000 and 10,000 years ago as part of the modern human tribe we call *Homo sapiens*. Obviously quite a bit had happened in terms of evolution in between Lucy and herself. Various human-type species had been and gone in several parts of the world, and science is still trying to piece together how that occurred. Although we would like it to be simple and neat, our evolutionary process seems to be more of a complex web of lineages than one straight-forward line of evolution.

In Tanzania, fossil footprints trailing across a lake date back to the *Australopithecines* and illustrate clearly that they were walking on two legs. Overlapping with Lucy's *Australopithecus afarensis* was *Australopithecus africanus* but they only lived in South Africa. Slender and with curved fingers for climbing, they seem to have vanished by 2.45 million years ago. There were other *Australopithecine* species throughout Africa, including the oldest, *A. anamensis*, which so far is only known about from fragments of jaws and teeth.

The *Australopithecines*, potentially, eventually gave way to the *Homo* genus. Three genera have emerged within that genus: *Homo*, *Kenyanthropus* and *Paranthropus*. *Homo* has usually been associated with the rise of tool use but the story and consequently the timeline is messy with debate, theory and conflicting evidence; some even suggest that *A. afarensis* were using stone tools a million years before *Homo* ever appeared. For the sake of simplicity here, what we do know is that *Homo habilis* appeared about 2.1 million years ago and was using tools. With some overlap, around 1.9 million years ago came *Homo rudolfensis*, who was larger and had a bigger brain, but there isn't much in the way of fossils. Probably also overlapping was *Homo erectus* who – with smaller teeth, a bigger brain and taller body – strode out of Africa, lost all their body hair and dispersed. From there we ended up with *Homo floresiensis*, a small-brained hobbit-like human, just over three feet tall, who lived on the island of Flores near Australia and only died out around 50,000 years ago. *Homo heidelbergensis*, fizzled out rather too – living between 700,000 and 200,000 years ago, they hunted, used fire and created shelters throughout Europe and Africa and parts of China.

Alongside all this were another group of hominids, the *Paranthropus* genus, including *P. boisei* discovered by Mary Leakey in 1959. This species had strong jaws and teeth and, significantly, lived alongside *Homo erectus*, flourishing in Africa for millions of years. *P. robustus* was much the same but lived in South Africa, and *P. aethiopicus* populated east Africa.

The Denisovan people of Asia were only identified in 2010 from a fossilised female finger bone but they appear to have died out, and so little is known about them that the debate still rages about where exactly they fit in.

Homo neanderthalensis disappeared about 40,000 years ago, having had a good crack of the whip. They used tools and hunted and even made offerings at graves, and they were our closest human relative. There is recent evidence to suggest that they interbred at times with *Homo sapiens* and that our population still contains Neanderthal genes as a consequence.

This all leaves us with *Homo sapiens* in more recent times – and with the job of trying to interpret evidence using a different paradigm from the one we are all too familiar with.

Lady Sapiens is crammed with evidence that women have been positively heroic, warrior-like and even revered and suggests that perhaps they didn't have to become like men to be that way. Rather than seeing women as domestic subordinates, this book paints a different story using a combination of palaeoanthropological studies, modern techniques like DNA sampling and pathology testing and also studying contemporary hunter-gatherer cultures – ethnoarchaeology. This story puts women in the centre of the frame as essential to the survival of the species, and not just because they were physically producing the babies. The authors seek to address the absence of women in the current narration of prehistory and suggest that different civilisations and cultures through time and space might have thought about women in a different way.

It's hardly outlandish to point out that these men would validate other men as the hunters and warriors that brought *Homo sapiens* to its crescendo. From painters to filmmakers to historians and scientists, the images of women reflect the paradigm of those depicting them. *Lady Sapiens* quotes Michèle Julien, Research Director Emeritus at the CNRS: 'The realities of life for prehistoric women are necessarily far removed from the nineteenth-century cliché we were given. Anthropological research has shown that, among all contemporary hunter-gatherers, women perform lots of activities – they are not sitting by the hearth breastfeeding the baby all day, waiting for food to be brought to them.' Interesting. Bang goes the greatest love story of all time.

First comes the idea that skull size relating to brain size is fair, but relating brain size to intelligence is not necessarily accurate. Early hominids had a brain size proportional to their skeleton size, therefore of course it was smaller – sexual dimorphism, duh! So devaluing the female by assuming that smaller size meant decreased intelligence was wrong.

Next comes the fact that numerous studies have shown, in both men and women of the Upper Palaeolithic, evidence of considerable upper-body strength. As we know, that doesn't just develop from sitting around breastfeeding and watching Netflix, it reflects the amount of physical activity it took to provide food for the group. Their diet was mostly vegetarian plus lean meat and there was little fat in anything they ate. As a consequence, they were likely muscular and lean, and evidence from teeth doesn't show that they were malnourished.

The discovery of elegant necklaces, beautifully carved antlers, teeth and shells – some of which had been transported many miles and sewn onto clothes, belts and bracelets – indicates that decorating the body and clothes was considered important. Pigments were transformed into paints and dyes, techniques that had to be developed and taught. Art was also considered important, beauty was valued, and desirability was a thing.

But what was a woman's place in society? For a community of humans to survive they had to be bonded and every member of that community would need to pull their weight, so it wouldn't make sense to exclude half the community (the female half) completely from the work of hunting for food. Evidence of baby carriers shows that mothers must have been freed up to work by having babies on their backs.

Grave sites have also revealed that many women were buried with special ornaments, weapons or jewellery, demonstrating the reverence with which they were treated even after their death. Surely these women contributed more than producing babies? Again there is no fossil evidence to go on, but the authors say there is no evidence to suggest that women weren't in positions of power either. We see matriarchal societies in whales and in elephants, so why not in humans too? Women could have been shamans, healers, artisans and even hunters. There is evidence from an archaeological site in Peru that a young woman was buried with everything she needed to hunt big game: all the tools were buried with her in a decorated satchel. Other sites have revealed the same thing: evidence that women – certainly in Peru between 12,000 and 8,000 years ago – were hunters too.

For me, one of the most interesting aspects of the book is the idea of using investigation of wear and tear of bones, and even studying the influence of the soft tissues on and around them, to reconstruct the daily tasks of a woman. Pathologies resulting from work-related stress were impossible a decade ago; now, it is much easier to see that repetitive work was a part of everyday life.

From the French authors of *Lady Sapiens* to anthropologists like Sarah Blaffer Hrdy (whose many books reveal a different aspect to mothers and evolution theories and what it is to be female), the challenges to our male-marinated prehistory and evolution are coming thick and fast. I don't doubt that the relative social value of child-rearing and associated domesticated activities to our species has been underrated by male historians, or that perhaps our female ancestors were up to far more with spears than we gave them credit for. In Germany, for example, scientists found the remains of a sabre-toothed cat in the same stratum as wooden spears on what would have been the bank of a shallow lake.[5] The layer was 300,000 years old. It can't be too much of a leap of faith to think that, given that type of lurking predator, a woman living on that lakeside with her family would make absolutely sure she was pretty handy with a spear too. Either way, what is certain is that women's relationship with nature in every facet was intimate and they had to be strong and capable to survive it.

Perhaps I'm not quite as unusual as I thought in my craving for wilderness and my hunger for adventure, or even my fascination with plants.

CHAPTER FIFTEEN

A Fascination for Plants

It's easy to forget that for the bulk of human existence plants were medicine. Using potions for healing isn't some magical interest that women had, some witchery that they developed; from our early existence, this would have been another practical way of taking care of the tribe, like hunting or creating fire. That wisdom would have been passed down orally. The smart people, those who learned well, had an ear for the details in others' suffering and would have been the ones who used those 'medicines' most successfully. Sounds pretty 'scientific' to me.

Liza's words echo in my ears: how long has there been a barrier between women and science? And was my theory that passion can outweigh any social constraints right? For centuries there was an outright prohibition of women in science (or anything much, for that matter). And there are the self-limiting barriers like fear. Can passion outweigh that? Or is it just that to be a 'wild woman' you actually need to be a special kind of person? A different type of person.

To have a relationship with the wild is, essentially, always going to be about having a relationship with fear. The wilderness, wild animals, and weather all test us, despite the magnificence of our evolution. Women are also tested in a different way, for women have had and still do have a reason to fear men. In the wilderness it is easy to conjure up an image of a strong man who might effortlessly overcome a woman. In civilisation the danger is often less obvious but has no less potential for harm, and is imbued in the very structure of society and the rules it imposes – the very culture of the way that 'civilised' women's lives play out. Perhaps perceived safety is part of the reason that, traditionally, many women prefer to stick to some kind of cultural norm.

The story of one eighteenth-century wild woman, Jeanne Baret, shows just how beautifully a passion for the natural world overrides any obstacle, even men. From her early days, Jeanne's first love affair was with plants. She grew up in rural France at a time when codes of behaviour and rules for what you could and couldn't do were dictated not only by gender but also by religion and class. In those early years, her mother inspired, fed and nurtured this passion in her smart young daughter. After all, in the culture she grew up in, this was not unusual for women – they used plants to heal and to cook with, and they knew all their properties. Jeanne was absorbing the oral tradition of women handed down through generations but, as they explored the fields and hedgerows around their village, neither of them would have had any idea where this love affair would take her. In the name of botany, Jeanne would be the first woman to circumnavigate the world, and she would do it in extraordinary circumstances.

Jeanne Baret lived as a botanist, an explorer, a traveller, a discoverer of species, and above all a woman of science who built upon her ever-expanding knowledge during decades of study. However, recorded history did not portray her that way. In fact, some of the men who were recording history at the time actually described her as a 'beast of burden'. On becoming familiar with her story, there are those who might claim that she would have been nothing without one particular man, yet you might also argue that this man might have amounted to very little, in the end, without her. Let me introduce you to Jeanne and the man in question and you can decide what exactly made Jeanne Baret a wild woman.

He was a middle-class, entitled, young Frenchman called Philibert Commerson. He had, by birth, access to an extremely comfortable lifestyle and an education. With all that came an ego and a wilful character that at some point had enabled him to decide on a rebellious stance: it was his life and he could do as he pleased, regardless of what the rules or culture he was surrounded by might dictate. He was also a man obsessed – not with Jeanne Baret (this is not really a romantic story) but with botany. He obstinately refused to become a lawyer or even a doctor, as directed by his parents. Instead he relentlessly chose plants: discovering them, naming them, growing them, analysing them, absorbing every cell of information he could, and meanwhile flouting any rule or obligation laid out before him. He was good at it, so good that he touched greatness, working with Carl Linnaeus, the great taxonomer himself, whose work and systems biologists the world over still rely on. Commerson was clearly marinading in the 'collect and classify' mentality of his time.

So, I'm guessing that when he met a young peasant girl working in the countryside, he had no hesitation in 'collecting' her. But time would tell that he struggled to properly 'classify' her, even by the end of his own life.

Despite being a 'not pretty but not plain' peasant girl when she met Commerson, Jeanne had a fine mind and curiosity and a great knowledge of plants stored in her brain. She must have been impressive for a man of his standing to want to overlook the fact that she was a peasant girl and therefore considered of no value in any way, certainly not intellectually. But hers was the kind of knowledge Commerson could not plunder from books because it wasn't yet in books. Instead it had been handed down by generations of women who intimately knew the properties and capabilities of the plants growing around them – which plants could abort a baby and which could heal pain, for example.

Perhaps they sensed in each other that mutual passion for plants.

When his wife died, shortly after their son was born, it was clearly inconceivable that a man like Commerson could take over running his own house and looking after his own child, so he employed his new 'peasant girl' friend, Jeanne, to do those things. We know little of their association before this, but the theory goes that they must have met and bonded over plants – probably working in the field. Commerson was clear: he never had any intention of marrying her but who was she to say no to the job of 'wife but not wife'? After all, the situation gave her a proper roof over her head, a meal and even a table to eat it on, and the chance of learning more as a botanist and working with plants in new ways. This was clearly a passion they shared and each had something to offer the other. Jeanne's knowledge helped Commerson set up a thriving business based around plant medicine, which must have worked well for him. (If my sarcasm is evident here, I make no apology.)

By all accounts, other servants noticed the somewhat unusual situation where the housekeeper had the freedom to come and go in her master's study, discussed his work with him and, judging by her increasing rotundity, presumably also had the freedom to come and go in his bed-chamber. When the murmurings of gossip turned into a groundswell of complaint, one might think that Commerson would do something about it – perhaps give up his peasant girl, find himself a new wife and mother for his son, and live a more fitting lifestyle – but Commerson was not about 'fitting' and perhaps not about caring much either. Instead, he handed his son to his brother-in-law to look after and hopped on a coach with his lover/housekeeper/fellow botanist/exploited peasant girl and made off for a new life in Paris. He would never see his son again.

Imagine that! Living in sin in Paris! How terribly modern . . . for the 1760s.

Jeanne must have been beside herself. Most peasants didn't get to stray much beyond their village in a lifetime, but here she was in a horse-drawn coach with the whole country laid out before her. And that was just the start of it. In return for his great kindness – or as a gesture of love – she gave Commerson a notebook full of her botanical knowledge, something of great value to him.

Paris turned out to be a great move. They lived in an apartment on the rue du Jardin – the 'jardin' being Paris's large botanic garden – and Jeanne was lucky enough to be able to tend to Commerson's every whim: keeping house, doing the shopping, studying and looking after the increasing collection of rare plants from the jardin. She met famous progressive scientists of the time, like Jean-Jacques Rousseau, and in December she still found the time to give birth to a baby.

After that things got a little wobbly.

For starters, the baby really got on Commerson's nerves. It's understandable: babies know nothing of stamens or sepals, species or Latin, and they have a real knack of disturbing the peace and distracting the mistress, I mean fellow botanist. Also the baby didn't seem to understand that Commerson had other stuff going on. He had far bigger fish to fry: fame was calling.

The French Royal Navy, on the command of the King, were planning a trip around the world. This was huge: they would be cocking their legs on 'territories' (other people's homes) all over the world. In the name of king and nation, they would be plundering the globe for resources to claim for themselves. It was all *très* exciting. There would be discoveries, adventure, the promise of naming new species, an on-deck pool and supper at the captain's table (actually, the on-deck pool might be my own flight of fancy). However, this was a chance in a lifetime for Commerson and he knew it. All he had ever dreamed of was being a botanist and plants – despite his parents, despite the cruel world that made him marry and earn a living. Even as a student, he had roamed the French wilderness in his passionate, rebellious state – despite causing himself injury on slippery rocks and catching rabies from a vicious dog that had bitten him on the leg. He had broken rules, stolen cuttings and given away his son; there was nothing he wouldn't do in the name of Commerson the Famous Botanist, and now the world would recognise his greatness.

Fuelled by botanical fervour and a big dollop of ego, the Commerson express train was en route from mid- to well-respected scientist to beloved hero of the nation via global circumnavigation. To keep the train moving, though, he would need an assistant – not a mother, and not a woman either because a woman on board a naval ship was highly illegal. No one really knows when the plan was hatched or whose idea it was, but the truth is that Commerson already had a very good assistant who was great at taking care of absolutely everything in his life – from tending and nurturing plants to taking care of him when he was ill (a familiar occurrence when things got tough). In fact, judging from the baby now wailing in the plant-filled apartment, she was perhaps *too* good at taking care of all his needs. My, what a hothouse they had created in the elegant apartment on the rue du Jardin.

Clearly the baby was a slight inconvenience to the Commerson express train, and so in January Jeanne did something that is almost inconceivable to most of us: she took her new baby son along to the Paris orphanage and handed him over. Again, we don't know if she thought this was a temporary measure, or whether it was her decision or Commerson's, but we do know that she never saw her little man again, as by December he was dead. And by then a young man called Jean Bart – assistant to Monsieur Commerson, botanist by royal appointment – was vomiting with the best of them on board the *Étoile*, one of two ships on the Royal French Navy trip destined to sail around the world.

It would be easy to keep writing Jeanne's story in this vein, but to do so would be to focus rather too much on Commerson and, while he would undoubtedly love that, I don't want to miss the buried treasure of the expedition.

It's not easy to ease ourselves into the mind of a peasant girl of the Dordogne but it might be easy to overlook her or underestimate her or simply see her as a being moulded by Commerson. Was it passion for him or for plants that drove her and gave her an adventurous spirit and boundless curiosity? Trying to work it out is like looking up at a rainforest canopy, where each leaf fills a space to harness the sunlight, and trying to distinguish individual trees – it's hard to know where one begins and ends and another takes over. But we do know what Jeanne was up against and that she was surely a one-off. Women of the time just didn't get opportunities like this, and they wouldn't have been culturally conditioned to take them anyway. They were expected to recoil, their feminine susceptibilities triggered at the very thought that plants might have reproductive organs. Botany was surely no study for a woman. Any woman who didn't recoil . . . well, there was obviously something very wrong with her. And no woman would be expected to voluntarily go through an arduous voyage with only 330 men – quite rough ones – for company. The very thought was scandalous. Women were – without a shadow of a doubt, and with the benefit of scientific knowledge – considered inferior both intellectually and physically.

Jeanne Baret was about to disprove all of that, to fly in the face of it, but it would cost her.

It wasn't long before suspicious glances turned to mumbling and unrest. Once again, when the murmurings of gossip turned into a groundswell of complaint, one might think that Commerson would do something about it. (A pattern is emerging . . .) Upon being called to the

Captain to discuss it, Commerson – guided by the stars of what he wanted rather than any kind of value system – did what suited him best in the moment and denied all knowledge of his assistant being a woman. The Captain, as had the crew, questioned him about the fact that his assistant was the only servant who ate and slept in his master's cabin rather than with the rest of the crew in their quarters. He observed the fact that Jean Baret was never seen at the 'heads' alongside the rest of the crew relieving himself or defecating, and this had the rest of the crew raising questions.

Commerson told the Captain that back in France he had failed to secure himself an assistant until just before the voyage, at which point a young man approached him at the dockside and they came to an agreement just in time. He had no prior relationship with the young man, Jean, but by this time was desperate to get someone.

The Captain requested that Jean sleep below decks with the crew. She did so, presumably slinging her hammock with gritted teeth and lying in it while tightly gripping a loaded pistol. When the inevitable advances began, she threatened to blow the head off any man who came too close. Like any woman, I can only imagine the fear she endured through those no doubt sleepless nights. The crew would not have had much respect for a woman who would willingly put herself in that situation and so for Jeanne what began as a deliberate flouting of rules, a desire to accompany Commerson, to see the world, to discover plants, must slowly have been turning into a darker journey.

The crew, knowing nothing of that fear, must have been super keen to get her to the equator; it was tradition for sailors to take part in a ceremony as the ship crossed from the northern to the southern hemisphere. Called 'Crossing the Line', it was conducted by a man dressed up as Neptune, involved stripping naked, being immersed in water, tarred

and feathered, possibly with a playful lashing around the
deck with the cat-o'-nine-tails, and generally being ridiculed
and abused. It was a 'rite of passage' designed to humiliate
for reasons only known to sailors of the time. Preparations
started days in advance and no crew member escaped it, so
neither would Jean. Then, the sailors must have thought,
they would know for sure whether they had a woman on
board.

From accounts written in various journals, we know that
Jean did not even remove 'his' top, for to do so would
expose a chest tightly bound in linens to disguise her
breasts. A pool was created for this ceremony, in the form of
a sail filled with sea water and excrement and trailed in the
sea. It was into this pool that the 'newbie' crew were
plunged. Not the officers, of course – the likes of
Commerson merely had to endure a bucket of water being
thrown at him and then it was pretty much over. He just
had to stand with the other officers and watch not only
Jean's humiliation but also her inability to get out of the
'pool' because, whenever she tried, she would be pushed
back down with long wooden oars brandished by the crew.
The rest of the newbies in the water no doubt used this
opportunity to thrash around and have a good underwater
grope in the search for the truth about the best gossip on
board. When the murmurings of complaint began to turn
into what must have been a groundswell of abusive
behaviour, one might think that Commerson would do
something about it. He didn't.

Finally the Captain confronted her. She, rather craftily,
hinted at a traumatic past, one that resulted in her becoming
a eunuch. Stories of sailors who had been kidnapped and
turned into eunuchs were a thing at that time and pretty
fear-inducing for the Captain and crew alike. So, for now,
she was relieved of the burden of any more questions. Not
long after that, the old dog bite on Commerson's leg
started ulcerating and he became ill so he requested that

Jean be moved back to his cabin to look after him, which I
guess would have been better than being below decks with
the gropers.

Being a woman was certainly coming at a cost. As the
voyage moved into the tropics, Jeanne's skin – under the
tight linen wraps that she could never remove – became
sore and full of eczema, which can't have been helped by
her dunk in excreta.

In Rio they finally had a chance to get botanising.
Commerson was frail again – but hey, he had Jeanne to
look after him, right? – and so, when they went on their
daily excursions from ship to shore to collect specimens,
they would only walk a short way together. Jeanne would
carry all the equipment, and Commerson would find
himself a nice spot to sit in while she went exploring and
collecting. During one of these solitary excursions she
found herself in a valley full of bougainvillea. These days
the colourful plant is known for its beauty, though some
people call it garish. To Jeanne, however, its seed pods
looked familiar – similar to French beans at home, which
could be used for their anti-inflammatory properties,
possibly to heal ulcers and sores – and so she collected
much of it presumably to help Commerson with his
ongoing difficulties (perhaps in the hopes that he would get
off his ass and actually help).

Commerson took full credit for the discovery, promptly
gave it its Latin name, and declared it discovered in Rio de
Janeiro in 1767. He then, smiling and full of generous spirit,
offered to name it after the Captain Bougainville. Never
mind the woman who found it, eh? Clearly not impressed
and ever more suspicious, Captain Bougainville took the
colourful boughs and the name credit and then placed
Commerson under house arrest in his cabin for a month for
clear rule flouting.

Still, the show must go on, and the voyage navigated
down the east side of South America, with Jeanne

collecting at every opportunity: wild fennel, agave, cacti, even beetles that might provide cochineal dye. The cabin filled up with boxes and specimens. They endured storms and starvation, she saw whales and phosphorescence and finally made it to the Strait of Magellan, where they would hopefully be able to navigate right through to the mysteries of the Pacific. This rather tricky navigation translated into a very slow boat ride with lots of stopping and starting, but that created the opportunity for many offshore expeditions during which Jeanne Baret met Patagonian tribes, walked through shores encrusted with elephant seals and penguins, and relentlessly collected plants, observing soil types and vegetation distribution and still carrying all the equipment. So hard did she work, in fact, that she earned herself that nickname 'beast of burden' (thanks, Commerson). Yet her physical capabilities must have also earned her the respect of the ship's crew because they were on board watching her as Commerson (once again sitting on his ass) directed her up and down scree slopes, around the rocky shorelines, up into forests and back down to the shore. Her dedication didn't waver, though, even as she dug up specimens using her bare hands, so she probably wasn't doing it for the love of Commerson.

On one occasion, when it looked like they might not get back to the ship for the night, the Captain ordered Jean to cut blocks of turf out of the frozen ground to build a temporary shelter while he stood by, watching and having a nice chat with Commerson. Let's not forget either how useful she was on board: half the crew had gonorrhoea and so she was busy collecting plants to help the ship's surgeon treat both that and scurvy. She really was a treasure. Meanwhile, during this part of the voyage Commerson managed to name a dolphin species after himself, even though that was not the done thing. It seems his ego really did know no bounds.

Safely through the Strait and out in the Pacific, they found Tahiti, which was a lovely surprise. No one from Europe knew it was there; although a British ship had recently landed and left, word hadn't got to the French yet. Interestingly, the Tahitians saw straight through Jeanne's disguise and, with no judgement, immediately declared her *māhū* (a person of the third gender). Transvestites being a common and much-loved part of their culture, they knew of no other reason a woman might dress as a man or vice versa. This must have only goaded the crew even more, but in the moment they were distracted by what were apparently orgiastic proceedings because they were having to fight off the Tahitian women who were allegedly throwing themselves at them. Commerson seemed to be indulging himself too, so Jeanne apparently trekked away from humans on shore or stayed in the cabin on board and in the safety of her world of work and plants.

Reading between the lines of the journals, it seems that after Tahiti events took a really dark turn for Jeanne. She was, shamefully, not to be left in peace to carry out her work. After months at sea, encounters with native peoples who did not welcome their visit or their show of superiority with a musket, violent storms, dwindling fresh water supplies and no food, which had the officers eating rats and the crew literally chewing on leather at mealtimes and starving to death, they finally went to shore at New Ireland. Here, according to some, she was 'inspected'; however, the truth is that she was almost certainly caught off guard without her pistol and assaulted and gang-raped. At home in France this would be a punishable offence, but who was going to tell? It was not in the interests of the Captain to have it reported at home because that would mean that either he had not even been aware enough to know there was a woman on board or he had done nothing about it. For Jeanne, aside from giving up a baby perhaps, it must have been the most traumatic of all the challenges she had so far endured under Commerson's watchful guardianship. From then on, no doubt suffering from PTSD, she stayed in the cabin.

The voyage went on to stop at the Spice Islands, where the Captain sent her ashore to try to collect valuable spices like nutmeg, but she didn't get anything owing to the watchful Dutch guards there. Then it was on to the busy hub port of Jakarta, where still she stayed on board, shutting herself in the cabin, because by then she must have realised she was two months pregnant – the timing clearly coinciding with the suspected rape.

Eventually the ship made land in Mauritius, which was French-owned at the time. Commerson and Jeanne were invited to stay, to move into the governor's residence and help him with discovering the fauna and flora of the island. Commerson would enjoy a guest suite and Jeanne would live in the servants' quarters. It must have been a huge relief for her to say goodbye for the final time to the crew and rapists of the *Étoile* and to have a safe room of her own for the first time in almost two years.

Time passed, another baby was given away, life in Mauritius was good and Jeanne no longer had to pretend she was a man. Funded by Poivre, the governor of Mauritius, the two botanists took a remarkable trip to survey nearby Madagascar. We now recognise Madagascar as a biodiversity hot spot and understand just how precious a part of our planet it is. Because it is a large island, and because of its geographical situation a few hundred miles off the coast of southern Africa, and because of its history (it split off from the African continent around 160 million years ago), subsequent 'independent' evolution makes Madagascar home to an extraordinary and unique range of endemic species – species that cannot be found anywhere else on Earth. According to WWF, approximately 95 per cent of Madagascar's reptiles, 92 per cent of its mammals and 89 per cent of its plant life is unique. Equally interesting because of its isolation are the amount of species that don't exist in Madagascar, particularly the large mammals.

Nowadays Madagascar is threatened by the usual culprits: as the human population has grown, deforestation is causing habitat loss and the illegal wildlife trade also endangers species like the chameleon. But in the 1760s, as Commerson and Jeanne walked around taking in the sights and smells of the forest, they would have had no idea of the impact of humans a few hundred years in the future. Madagascar must have been mind-blowing for both of them. They collected hundreds of specimens, and Commerson – now perhaps moved by guilt – finally named a genus after her: '*Baretia*'. Sadly, it no longer bears her name but it was an interesting choice; not only does it have a long history of being used for medicinal purposes, but each plant contains a range of leaf shapes and sizes so it is pretty hard to identify it as one thing. Perhaps Commerson saw a similarity with the peasant girl/ lover/botanist/woman who strode beside him wearing men's clothing only because she now found it to be practical in the forest.

Back on Mauritius, the governance changed. Where Commerson and Jeanne had been revered and respected by the previous governor, the new governor had little interest in their work. Suddenly in a position of having to fund themselves, they bought a lowly house in the port to share with their valuable collection. They lived there for a year before Commerson became very ill again – he had rheumatism and dysentery and, in March 1773, an abscess burst in his chest and he died. Considered no more than a servant, Jeanne was not permitted back in her own house and her treasured collection was impounded by the government and sent to France – she never saw it again.

She ended up working in a tavern, and that's where it could have ended, but happily this was not the conclusion to her story. A year later she married. Her new husband was a soldier in the French army and permitted to claim passage with his new wife back to France and so, late in 1774, with no welcoming committee and no recognition of what was actually happening, Jeanne Baret stepped back onto French soil, the first woman to circumnavigate the globe.

She claimed her rights to Commerson's will and had enough to buy herself and her new husband a comfortable home. And in 1786 she began to receive a pension from the Royal Navy: 200 livres per year, the exact same amount that would be given to a man of science. Was it in recognition of her work? Was it merely in lieu of Commerson and his will? Was it lobbied for by the same captain who had permitted unpunished rape and cruelty in order to preserve his own good name? We don't know.

Jeanne lived a married life in rural France until her death at 67, but another gap in our knowledge of her is how her travels and work affected her and what she did. Commerson plucked Jeanne from the hand-to-mouth existence of a French peasant with a potential lifespan of around thirty years, and she became a self-assured, financially independent scientist who travelled around the world and lived into her sixties. Or did she pluck herself?

In a rare, if unique, credit to her from a fellow passenger on the *Étoile*, Prince Nassau-Siegen wrote in his journal: 'I want to give her all the credit for her bravery, a far cry from the gentle past-times afforded her sex. She dared confront the stress, the dangers, and everything that happened that one could realistically expect on such a voyage. Her adventure should, I think, be included in a history of famous women.' Glynis Ridley, who has researched and documented Jeanne's life and provided me with much of the information you have just read, notes: 'The reality of what happened to Jeanne Baret on New Ireland was a human trauma that screams for recognition, a lone powerless terrified woman who was violated emotionally, psychologically and physically. When sexual violence is added to the catalog of conditions within which she lived and worked, it only enhances the nature of her achievement,' and I don't think I could sum it up any better.

Without a shadow of a doubt, Jeanne lived in a male-dominated society in which it was very difficult to escape the boundaries of class, and so without Commerson she would never have had the opportunities she did. But what of her work? After all, she didn't set out to be the first woman to circumnavigate the world. Her life simply followed a trail that the plants laid before her. Her reason to keep going through all the darkness remained the collection that she gathered and labelled. She organised, examined and pressed specimens – hundreds and hundreds of plants in all their wonderful forms from seed to bract and stem to petal. That collection perhaps was her one true love. To reduce a woman's life to her romances is one thing, but love and passion are part of women and if this woman's tale is in any way a romantic one then surely it is for the collection that she struggled rather than for Commerson. I cannot imagine her grief when on the dockside of Mauritius she was no longer given access to her collection, and instead had to watch, powerless, as it was shipped to France without her.

In Paris her work survived the Revolution and some of it, even now, is in the French national herbarium and seed banks, so – on top of an extraordinary achievement – she left an enduring legacy. Bougainvillea now climbs and flowers all over the balustrades and gardens of Europe and it is as much associated with the Mediterranean as it is with South America. From now on, when I see it I will think not of Bougainville nor of Commerson but of Jeanne Baret, a young French peasant woman who found herself sweaty, sore and itchy, her chest tightly bound, in man's clothes, laden with botany equipment but alone, free from prying eyes for a moment, in a wild valley near Rio de Janeiro, in awe of a brand-new beautiful plant.

SPRING

CHAPTER SIXTEEN

Knowing My Place

A long bank stretches from the kitchen up the garden. When we first arrived it was nothing but flat conifers. Straight out of a low-maintenance gardening manual, they had no place in my vision of an English country garden alive with flowers and tradition and native species, and these particular conifers had zero value to wildlife that I knew of. Even back then, before it had become a thing, I was fully aware that I wanted to fill the garden with pollinator-friendly flowers. So out came those flat, ugly, pine-dropping plants. Over the years, instead, I gradually planted bulbs: snowdrops, daffodils, bluebells and − even though they weren't completely natural to the place − tulips.

The tulips were particularly memorable. Post-caesarean, with a dodgy intensive care moment and a full blood transfusion under my belt, I was advised against any exercise for a while. However, the large sack of tulips I had ordered on special offer months earlier had finally arrived, the sun was shining on a bright autumn day, and I was going out of my mind being cooped up inside and barely moving. So, envisaging a bank of bright dancing tulips, I tucked the baby into the pram for his nap and we both headed outside.

'I'm taking it easy, I promise,' were my departing words.

Getting down on the ground was slightly more excruciating than I had thought it might be, so once I got down I decided it was best to stay down. Inching my way up the flower-bed on my hands and knees was easier, the earth's smell rose up to me and I felt my spirits rise with each newly buried bulb. It was worth it, despite the odd wince. All I had to do was imagine the colourful swathe of tulips blooming in the spring and I found I was able to inch along a bit more.

The following spring, though I waited with bated breath, not one bright tulip came up. I'm guessing squirrels were the burglars but we shall never know for sure. Yet, over the years, what did come up was snowdrops, then daffodils, then bluebells. I thought about that bank quite often while we were in the States. Where daffodils in the UK flag up the return of spring early in the year, in Wyoming they wait until May. Only then do they feel confident enough to leave the frozen ground and open themselves up to the fact that winter might finally be over and the snow gone for a little while. It always seemed like such a long wait.

In my absence, things here had changed. What started as a little clump here and there had now become an extraordinary spread. Nature had simply taken my project and run with it, giving me both the comforting thought of what it is capable of over time and a significant return on my bulb planting investment. A blanket of white snowdrops now completely covered the bank, and there was no time for sorrow as it faded because it was closely followed by the bright spears and yellow heads of so many daffodils and then, just a few weeks later, the blue haze of bluebells.

I felt it again – a homecoming, a somehow reassuring sense that I had merely helped something that would carry on with or without me. It was nature saying, 'Thanks, small person, I'll take it from here. Stand back, though, because you might be pretty impressed.' This spring-filled bank was no mountain vista, but in the same way it put me in my rightful place and that felt good.

CHAPTER SEVENTEEN

Surviving Motherhood

Back and forth goes my jumbled mind, from memory to memory, year to year. Spring in Wyoming, where we weren't the only ones coming out of what felt like a long hibernation; bears were too. And this was usually when they were most irritable and hungry, so you really didn't want to get in their way.

Grizzly bears are associated with the wilderness in our minds as a form of danger. And that is completely valid – they are. While checking camera traps in remote areas of the Grand Teton National Park, there was nothing more fear-inducing than a large, fresh grizzly footprint, or a brown furry body lurking in the trees. Those kinds of moments are when you know a little of what it is to be truly wild – when, as Liza said, you suddenly find yourself completely 'in the moment'. A little flurry of adrenaline accompanies the knowledge that you could be hunted here, eaten, that you are just a human.

Grizzlies instil fear in us for good reason. In my time living in Jackson Hole, we heard regularly of people making a silly mistake and getting attacked for it. Most recently it was someone who lived near to us. In the pre-dawn, he and his fellow hunter had returned to their elk carcass after leaving it overnight. They were bent over, butchering the carcass, and didn't even have time to reach for their bear spray when they were attacked by a female coming out of the vegetation at high speed. The presumption was that she must have been feeding on their carcass and they disturbed her when they returned. One man was killed, leaving behind a young family.

I had some encounters myself. One was on a fine spring day when the Grand Teton National Park had just opened the roads to cyclists. Through winter, these wonderful roads that wind around the park are impassable, deep in snow. The only way to travel them is by cross-country ski. Every year, for a couple of weeks at the start of the spring, the roads are opened up for cyclists only. It's a moment to be celebrated, a sign that the long Wyoming winter is releasing its grasp and will soon relinquish itself to spring. Ploughed clear of several feet of snow, the roads are now blank beautiful trails wending through the mountains, inviting us to enjoy the peace before the visitors come. Along with the chill, now there is a thrill in the fresh air, and the chance at last to get out on a bike ride alongside the lakes and through the snow-clad pine forests, with the bonus that you don't have to share the road with one car or coach.

Ten miles in and three of us, myself and two new friends, are all feeling good until a group of men in lycra overtake us, super speedy and silent. As a group of women, we are slower – not because of diminished athletic ability, of course, but because an important part of the outing for us is talking, bonding and laughing. We discuss kids, and the much-estimated defrosting of Jackson Lake – every year bets are taken: when would the thick white, snow-covered ice thaw and the waters turn turquoise under the Wyoming sky? It wouldn't be long now. We pull up at the junction for Jenny Lake and String Lake to decide whether we should take the longer route. Standing with our bikes between our legs, taking in the view and swigging icy water from our bottles, we are in no rush. Our conversation turns to another spring subject, something else that wouldn't be far away: when would the grizzly bears wake up? Between slugs of water, Jen and Caroline – both women who live pretty remotely – confess that it is the only thing about spring that they mind.

'It just makes my commute so much more challenging,' says Caroline, shoving her water bottle back into its holder and taking her helmet off to wipe the sweat from under her blonde bangs. 'I mean, I understand bear jams, I understand why people would stop the car to look at a bear and I still love seeing them, but I see them most days and I just need to get to school.'

Caroline is the headmistress of Moran School. When my two youngest joined, it brought the total register of children to sixteen. It is one of the more remote schools, an hour's drive from the main town of Jackson and where grizzly bears have been known to appear in the playground.

'For me, it's just that they are always hanging around outside our home,' says Jen, who then lived just inside the National Park. 'Last year, we had to stay in the car for an hour, waiting for a bear to leave, before we could get into the house. And then I was so scared getting the kiddos out of their car seats in case it came back, so I was staggering up the path but I just didn't want to put little Anna down.'

We laugh with her. On one level the image is funny, that scramble of fear. I vividly remember as a child swimming in a frenzy, going as fast as I could to the safety of shore on Bournemouth beach, just because my imagination convinced me that there was a shark in the water below. But here the fear is justified. Here it is not the work of an overactive imagination. Grizzly bears are sometimes unpredictable, but they are especially so in spring. They have just woken from hibernation and are hungry, and sows (female bears) are often bringing new cubs from the safety of their den into the big wide world for the first time. I remember taking my baby home from the hospital and being terrified that other drivers would career into our car – I can only imagine what it must be like to monitor three little toddling bear cubs in the world.

'It would be funny if it weren't so scary,' says Jen, 'but only a few minutes after we got into the house, that bear was back in the yard and the kids were pointing at it through the window. And while I was freaking out, they started laughing at me!'

We clamber back on our bikes, comment on the crystal air and the sharp Teton mountains reaching high into the blue sky. We're all excited about the next leg of the ride, an easy flat loop to revisit the clear lakes and the scents of the pine forest. So it takes a moment for us all to realise that what we are seeing is real.

The bear explodes out of the trees to the left of us, around six hundred brown furry, muscular pounds, racing across the snow towards us. I know that a grizzly can hit speeds of 35mph. I know that but I have never witnessed it before, and those two things are very different. It seems as though this bear is almost flying. I also know immediately that the bear is running way faster than I can cycle.

We brake to a dramatic halt and fall silent. Knowing we will look bigger, and feeling a sudden need to, we stand closely together, all of us thinking the same thing: 'Is he actually heading for us or were we just in his way?' Stopping means that, instead of intersecting with us, he is now headed for the road slightly ahead of us. Another few yards of cycling, or if we hadn't seen him, we would have crashed right into him.

I'm pretty sure I'm not even breathing. At his current rate, he will be at the road in a second.

I breathe again when it becomes clear that, even if he had noticed us, he wasn't interested. He didn't slow a touch for the road but careered straight across it, bowling through the deep snow bank on the other side as if it were nothing, and disappearing into the forest.

That is when the fear really kicks in. What is he doing now? Is he circling back to find us? Has he carried on?

'Should we stay still or ride?'

None of us wants to look like prey on the run at this point.

'Stay still.'

'Can you see him?'

'No, I can't hear him either.'

'Should we turn around?'

None of us has an answer because none of us knows where that bear is and we are all so struck by the fact that there is no way we could out-speed him, even wearing lycra, even on our road bikes.

Then we hear an engine behind us. A truck. We don't have time to wonder what a truck is doing on the road when it is just meant to be us cyclists, but nor do we care. The large grey truck – typical of the kind that Americans drive in Wyoming, wide enough to get stuck in a London street – pulls up behind us.

'You ladies see that bear?' calls a man's voice.

I want to laugh. What does he think? Why does he think we are standing there?

'Yes,' calls Caroline, 'can you see him now?'

Oh, how we longed for the safety of that truck.

'No, he's gone into the trees.'

'We weren't sure whether to turn around or just stay put.'

'I'll tell you what, I'll drive alongside you and put the truck between you and the trees just until we get clear of the area. That way, if he is circling round, he won't be able to see you.'

So that is what we do – with eyes on stalks, hyper-vigilant the whole way – because from the millisecond you have children, you find yourself far more cautious in a different way about any risk that might remove you from your ability to care for them, especially the kind of risk that might eat you.

If there is one thing about being female in particular that changes everything, it's motherhood. It defines us whether we want it to or not, whether we embrace it or push it away; the ability to have and nurture and need to protect offspring changes everything. In the animal world there isn't really a choice about whether or not you allow this biological function to play out. In fact, you could argue that the reason we don't seem to observe existential crises in the animals of the natural world is because 'the reason for being' is quite clear: survive to reproduce, replication of genes. Kind of a game-changer in its simplicity. If conditions are good enough – diet, habitat, stress not too high – reproduction will occur. Job done, life happening. Beautiful landscapes, meaning and purpose, ego – none of those things really comes into it. No one even compares dens (although there is a little competition in some bird species for a partner with decent nest-building abilities). And so we come to the peculiar challenges faced by the female gender. The curious combination of grit and tenderness required to nurture babies while surviving, the evolutionary advantages that have been granted us to do so, and how that may affect what being wild looks like for the female of the species.

The bear I most often encountered was a mum in the wilderness, bear 399 (the name once given to her by a research team). I wrote about her in *On the Trail of Wolves*. She is the most famous bear of the Greater Yellowstone Ecosystem, possibly in the world. Since I wrote about her, she has further astounded humans not only with her longevity but also with the way she rises ever more to the challenge of motherhood in the gruelling wilds of Wyoming. She was born in 1996, so as of 2023, that makes her twenty-seven, and I know that she is currently asleep hibernating in a den, north of Jackson. Over her extraordinary lifetime, 399 has been a model mother of eighteen cubs. She has had three sets of triplets and two sets of twins, along with just single cubs in some years. Because she has always roamed the same territories in and around Grand Teton National Park just south of Yellowstone, we have an exquisite amount of data on her life. Grizzly bears stay with their mum for around two and a half years. There is a lot to learn if they are to survive as adults, so two summers are spent learning how to find food and the winters are for hibernating.

The spring I lived there, I would watch her lead her triplets over the valley, teaching them how to be bears, watching patiently as they approached horses in a paddock and realised they wouldn't tolerate any mischief. Showing them how to use their long claws to dig up food, how to use a telegraph pole to scratch a back itch, how to take down an elk calf and how to cross a road.

But 399 has been a visible bear too. In 2004 she lost her first cub when it was still small (it wasn't known whether that was from starvation or an encounter with another bear or maybe even wolves) and since then she has been pretty visible to humans and stayed close to roads. It is thought that this strategy isn't a coincidence but rather a smarter form of childcare – that mums with young cubs often feed close to the road because it protects them from attack from male bears. Male bears will kill and eat young if they get in the way of a potential mating opportunity, and they take no part in raising their young. Her strategy has made her a high-profile bear, and that comes with a higher risk from humans.

Even more recently, 399 has shown just how flexible, smart and determined you have to be to survive not just as a wild mama but a wild mama of four. By 2020, as bear fans across the valley waited for her to emerge from her winter den, it was widely presumed that she would be alone, that her birthing days were done. She is getting quite old now and it's rare for a bear to give birth beyond their mid-twenties, so it was a surprise when she emerged with not just one cub but four. She also found herself with a lot of challenges: did she feel her age? Was her hunting edge going? Feeding and teaching a family of four cubs would be a phenomenal feat, but was she fit enough to pull it off?

By summer of 2021 those four cubs were almost grown, which meant they needed even more food. We don't know whether it was that, the extraordinary amount of tourists in the park, the low water levels in Jackson Lake, or other factors but something made 399 leave the normal confines of her territory and head towards the town of Jackson Hole. She was spotted in residential areas and gardens as she swept through the outer reaches of town, and the large family ended up in the wilderness south of town for a time in late summer, one day surprising a local horse rider on the trail who managed to capture the brief encounter on her iPhone before her horse Rooster turned and cantered her all the way back to the safety of their truck.

Local people were urged to give the bear family space and not to document their whereabouts on social media. Now, perhaps more than any time for 399, the main danger came from humans. If conflict arose either with her or one of the cubs, if they became too dependent on human food sources, they would need to be euthanised as they would become too dangerous. This was not the time for 399 to start teaching her cubs about human food sources, however desperate they may be, because it would lead to disaster. Yet again, she proved she is a smart bear, making it a 'lifestyle choice' to bring cubs around humans and to survive that by not causing conflict. She teaches her cubs those lessons along the way – and on the whole they are good lessons as, so far, this survival method has worked for her. The future risk, though, is that these cubs become too accustomed to being close to humans and get into trouble once they are young adults and away from her watchful gaze. Plus there is the ever-present threat that grizzlies are taken off the endangered species list and hunting starts up again; at that point, if they go out of the park, they might not be lucky enough to avoid a trophy hunter.

By the autumn, 399 and her cubs had come closer to transgressing the rule that they could not possibly know: in their desperation to take on as many calories as possible ahead of winter, they had fed on cattle-feed and raided five beehives but, although this was now becoming a concern, they had so far not eaten human food, bird food or pet food, or anything from a non-natural source. The bears were being watched and, in order to protect them from temptation, the whole county was reminded not to put trash out overnight and to make sure any food source – from BBQs to bird food – was secure.

By November, the decision was taken to radio-collar two of the cubs. Any interference comes with a risk but it was considered more important that they were closely monitored. At the same time, 399 was taking her own calculated risk in going nearer humans, nearer town, out of the park. Did she know that they might find more food that way – enough to feed five for the upcoming winter – or was it forced by lack of food in the park? Was this a new pattern for her, something she had done secretly before, or something she only chose to do out of dire necessity because she had four cubs and perhaps was losing the energy of her youth?

Whatever the decision-making process, in mid-November, 399 decided it was time to head back up north to home territory. Of course, she made the headlines doing it. Rather than take a circuitous or subtle route, the family of five huge bears took their time and a direct line right through the middle of Jackson Hole town. They strolled along the road past my old house, then up for a little meander across the elegant lawn and sculptures at the Center for the Arts, before being caught on a security camera walking brazenly across the car park at the police station. The family were then escorted out of town by law enforcement and made it home to the wilderness and a winter bed.

After what felt like a longer than normal wait, 399 broke all records and expectations, no one thought that she would have another cub, and many thought that she would never emerge from hibernation again, but emerge she did with one tiny cub – surely a breeze after being a single parent of four. This female can survive both wilderness and humans, and clearly has the intelligence to adapt to changing circumstances and do things her own way. She does this alone – no village, no husband, no matriarchal herd – so I would argue that the ability to not only survive in the wilderness but also to rear so many cubs flies in the face of the idea that females are weakened by their reproductive functions. Especially when you get curious about what a male grizzly does in any one year by comparison.

CHAPTER EIGHTEEN

When Doing What it Takes Doesn't Work

Not all sows are so lucky. Not all females are as wild-smart, and not all bears are as familiar with the landscape they find themselves in.

In July 2010, a mother bear and her three cubs wandered along the shallow banks of a small fast-running creek. The wide, grassy valley spread to either side, opening up the vast blue sky, the water gurgling as it navigated over and around the large grey rocks littering the river's bed. The sow was thin, hungry. She was always hungry – as were her yearling cubs, born the spring before last. However much they searched, there never seemed to be enough food for the three of them. The previous summer, while the cubs were still small, it had been easier but now they were almost fully grown and they never seemed satisfied.

The scents of humans were in this place, something the sow wasn't easy with. In the mountains they had rarely encountered them, and then only from a distance. When they had passed a human building, the bear didn't know whether or not to be alarmed. The humans she saw stayed at a safe distance, so she ushered her cubs forward, heading quickly down the riverbanks to the wide plains where there was only grass, rocks and trees as far as she could see and plenty of water to cool her family on this hot day.

Now they were going slowly again, searching for food. The cubs were getting more skilled at using their long claws to dig into the dry earth, searching for grubs and roots, but the sow knew they needed more than that to eat. They needed meat. Somewhere in this area was a bear she knew so, perhaps she reasoned, this must be a good place for bears.

According to several observations, the bear family spent the next few weeks exploring. The sow perhaps got used to

the scents and sounds of the humans in the distance and so
maybe they no longer bothered her as they were never a
threat. Leaving the valley, they explored the forest, searching
for food the whole time.

Only on one day did they come really close to a human,
when she allowed her cubs to step out onto the road. The
sow had encountered roads since she was a cub, and they
had criss-crossed this road a couple of times now with
nothing to worry about. So on this one day, with no sound
of vehicles, she led her cubs right out onto it. As soon as
they left the safety of the trees she saw a human running
towards them – alone but running and too close.

The sow stood up on her hind legs immediately, matching
the human's height and more, a warning not to come closer.
Seeing her, the human stopped running but stared,
challenging her with eye contact. Fear filled the sow, the
instinct to protect her cubs. She had to send a clear message:
keep away. Falling to all fours, her legs stiffening with
adrenaline, she charged.

The human yelled at her. High-pitched sounds: 'Hey!
Hey! Hey!' The noise brought her to a halt, suddenly unsure.
Then the human took a step back – the charge had worked.
In an instant, the sow decided to quit while she was ahead
and still had some distance, and so – with a quick grunt at
her cubs, commanding them to head into the forest – she
gave one more look at the human and then turned away,
pushing the cubs into the safety of the thick trees. If she had
looked back then, she would have seen the human turn and
run in the opposite direction, away from them. She had
won. Soon the family were back to searching for scraps of
food on the cool forest floor as if nothing had happened.

Perhaps she could be less fearful of humans now, which
was good because they seemed to be everywhere, not just
on the roads but in the most unexpected places. In a clearing
close to the creek, they found a place where humans must
often come and go, a place full of enticing food smells that

the cubs enjoyed investigating, but there was no actual food to be found. The sow was still wary and so, when another carload of humans approached, they returned to the safety of the trees and, unseen, watched the humans eat.

In these hot days, they spent time between the forest and the creek to stay cool. Yet, increasingly, the sow felt weak, her belly was sore, her breath shallow and her cubs ever demanding. They needed meat but she didn't have the energy to hunt. The one time she could rest was if they caught themselves up in rough-and-tumble matches, wrestling, play-fighting, learning about their strength, ready for the day when they might have to fight for real. As she sat on her haunches to watch them, her stomach pained her, she felt breathless, her old energy lacking, yet all her focus had to be on keeping the cubs moving and finding more food, keeping them safe.

Occasionally they scented that other bear, the one that seemed familiar to her. One night they even came close to finding him. His scent led them to a place where humans were, so the sow was a little nervous, but the humans were all sleeping. The enticement of new food smells in this place was too hard to resist and the sow allowed the cubs to explore. They came across a huge hard box. Although it smelled as though it might contain all the food their hunger craved, they couldn't work out how to get into it. They padded around and around it and they clawed at it from every angle but, try as they might, they couldn't break through the tough exterior so, after a while, they reluctantly gave up.

She led them away, huffing a little with frustration. They were closer than she wanted to be, passing right by the sleeping human bodies as they lay in strange structures, sealed against the night. She paused for a moment, though, savouring another smell that came from some of them. It was a good smell – the strong scent of fish, which made her mouth water. The sow and her cubs had been living an almost completely vegetarian diet for too long. She wondered if it might be worth coming back here. She wondered about the fish she could smell and how to get it.

'However, none of these issues can be identified as a causative factor for this bear to suddenly become predatory on humans.' – Report on the Soda Butte campsite attack 2010.

I was sitting in Jan's Café in Cooke City, drinking hot, thick coffee as the snow fell outside. Jan Gaertner and I had been talking about wolves, as I was writing my wolf book at that time, but we also discussed bears and the tragic story that had unfolded for a mother bear who was new to the area.

'It was in the very early hours of a hot July morning,' Jan said. 'The phone woke me up with a jump but, when you're part of the local emergency medical response team and you are on call that night, it shouldn't really be that surprising. I had been fast asleep, though, so really my brain was still coming to while I was getting dressed and being briefed on the phone at the same time. I heard the word "attack" and said, "OK, heart attack?" to confirm but what really woke me up was the reply. "No," said my colleague, "bear attack!"'

At this moment, despite living in the small town of Cooke City just outside Yellowstone National Park, Jan stepped into the unknown. She had never before dealt with a bear attack.

'I was shocked,' she said. 'Not in twenty years of being here as a first responder had I heard those words on a call-out. But that was just the beginning; I had no idea of what we were in for that night.'

As instructed, Jan ran over to the Super 8 motel, where they would be treating the patient. The patient had come from the Soda Butte Campground, just a mile away and five miles east of the north-east entrance to Yellowstone. It isn't a big campsite, just room for twenty-seven tents. The tents are spaced out in clearings between the spruces and conifers, giving each some privacy, but linked by a winding track. The site has the usual 'bear-proof' food storage facilities to be found in any campsite in the Yellowstone area: huge metal boxes with heavy, latched lids.

People do come to Yellowstone in the hope of spotting bears; both grizzly and black bears are known to live here, and sometimes they are spotted in the Soda Butte campsite. Only a few days before the attack, a photograph was taken of a young bear near the food storage with a distinctive white 'collar' marking. Sometimes just their footprints are seen. Campers often report hearing them in the night. In fact, only that morning a young lad who was camping with his parents had told them that he heard a bear moving around in the darkness of the previous night – but they thought it might be a tall tale and put it down to an overactive imagination.

Jan was briefed that a young man, Ronald Singer, had been sleeping in the tent he was sharing with his girlfriend and their young dog, when he was bitten, through the canvas, on his lower leg. He had no idea what was going on but, in his shock, he had the presence of mind to punch hard at the animal that had its teeth in his leg, which did the job – the bear left.

'I had never seen injuries like it,' Jan told me. 'Really deep laceration and puncture wounds. We were concerned that the leg might be broken because of the force of the attack, and the muscle wounds were so deep. It was shocking, but at that point you don't have time for shock or to even think about or wonder at it; your entire focus is on your job – getting the wounds treated, stopping the bleeding and getting the patient as stable as possible while we wait for emergency transport to the best hospital.'

'And what does emergency transport mean out here?' I asked.

'Well, sometimes a helicopter,' she replied with a wry grin, 'but it was the middle of the night, and this time his family actually drove him there.'

Ronald Singer had woken seconds before he was bitten, because the tent was moved several feet by the force of a bear trying to get in. Then he felt the animal bite into his leg through the canvas and – perhaps because he was a young man and a wrestler – his first reaction was to punch and yell. It made the animal let go of him. After that, he looked through the rip in his tent but in the darkness there was no sign of what had attacked him.

'But that wasn't the worst of it,' Jan said, 'we already knew that the bear had attacked again. You see, Ronald and his girlfriend had family in a nearby tent. Between Ronald yelling and his girlfriend screaming during the attack, they all woke up and came to his aid. There is no cell service in the camp so they loaded up in the car to drive here to Cooke City and dial 911 but, as they were doing that, they heard a woman screaming in another part of the camp. So we were pretty sure we might be dealing with two attacks, but we had no details on the second one.'

I wondered why the Singer family hadn't stopped to find out more.

'It wasn't long before we got our next patient – Debbie Freel,' Jan continued.

Debbie had been sleeping alone in her tent when she was attacked, because apparently, she had sent her husband to sleep in his own tent. The bear had moved along the row of tents, skipping two before it decided to attack again. Debbie came in with wounds to her left arm and leg. Right away she said that she thought she had heard a bone break – and she was right: she had a broken ulna and wounds that went deep into the muscle. Some were 15cm long. She said that when the bear had hold of her arm it felt like a vice just getting stronger and stronger, tighter and tighter. She had bear spray right there in the tent next to her, but it was a couple of inches out of reach. She screamed and the bear shook her and let go but then bit down into her lower arm, which was when she heard her bone break. At that point she figured it was best to play dead. The bear then bit her lightly on her leg without causing any damage and disappeared. She said there was a lot of noise in the camp by that point, so perhaps that was what scared it off. It was later discovered by the investigating team that the bear had clamped down on her arm so hard that it broke a tooth.

'It was pretty quick that the team were assembled and they headed down to the site to evacuate it,' Jan said, shaking her head at the memories. 'We didn't know much about what was going on at that end because our biggest concern was getting Debbie stable while we waited for the ambulance to arrive and take her to the hospital. Then I was asked to come to the campsite in case there were any more victims. So I rode there with James Miller, a Montana game warden. By the time we got there they had found another, third victim but there was nothing for me to do – the bears had already killed this guy. They had dragged him out of his tent, it seems by his head and shoulders, and killed him. By the time they found him, most of his torso had been eaten. It was unbelievable.'

It was as though the bear went from tent to tent, 'learning' what to do. She started with legs and then arms and finally worked out to go for the head.

'Why did she attack some tents and not others?' I asked.

'That we just don't know, and we couldn't work it out,' Jan said, 'although we have one theory, but we didn't come up with that until much later.'

Sometime between 2am and 4am, Kevin Kammer, who was sleeping alone, was dragged from his tent by the head and shoulders and killed. Much of him was eaten. The waters of Soda Butte creek, running along the south side of the campground, create a high level of ambient sound that makes hearing noises in adjacent campsites difficult. The nearest neighbours were camping sixty yards away, and they hadn't heard a thing.

Meanwhile, according to the report published later,[1, 2] officials were arriving: first, a team from the Sheriff County office came, then they were joined by Montana Fish and Wildlife wardens and Park Game Wardens, along with officials from Yellowstone National Park and the US Forest Service. The campsite was evacuated and the entrance guarded. The crew collected evidence, hair samples for DNA from the attack sites and the body, photographs. A plane was sent up to check for telemetry signals for collared bears in the area but found none. Quite quickly, it became obvious that there was more than just one bear involved. Footprints around Kevin Kammer's tent showed a large set of prints and many smaller ones. Scats, containing nothing but vegetable matter, were clearly from an adult and possibly more than one smaller bear.

Now the hunt was on to catch the bears before they could strike again. Culvert traps were baited and set. A culvert trap is like a giant stainless steel pipe, so called because they mimic a culvert or drainpipe big enough for a grizzly to comfortably fit into. One end is sealed shut and the other has a trapdoor. Once the bear pulls on the bait at the innermost point of the trap, the door behind them closes before they can turn around. The largest trap was set just six feet away from where Kevin died. It was baited with bighorn sheep meat and then covered with the flysheet of his tent. After the work was done, at around 3.30pm, everyone left the site.

At 6pm the door on the largest culvert trap closed – an adult grizzly was inside, a large female. She was immobilised, and samples of hair, blood and tissue were taken for DNA sampling. The crew also saw that she had recently broken her upper right canine tooth, and it matched the tooth found in Debbie's tent.

While the work was carried out, three smaller bears were seen hanging around in the willows at the edge of the stream. They were captured in culvert traps that night and then the whole family was taken a few hours away to Bozeman, on the other side of the national park, where – as soon as it was confirmed that her DNA matched that of the attacking bear – the sow was euthanised. Her three cubs, having known the taste of human flesh, would never be able to live wild again and so they were taken to ZooMontana to spend the rest of their lives in captivity.

There was DNA evidence of another bear: a fifth bear related to the sow, just one hair on one shoe. This bear was almost certainly not involved in any of the attacks but must have been hanging around the area and the campsite at some point.

'So what is that theory, Jan? Why on earth would she attack some tents and not others?'

'Well, she was no doubt travelling along the river side of the campsite. That is no surprise – all sorts of wildlife use that creek as a travel corridor. This bear and her cubs had been seen by a warden when she was travelling down that river in Yellowstone. The campsite was clean, there was no food stuff left anywhere, and everyone had followed the rules precisely. Debbie Freel had not even used any lotions or scents and had changed clothes before going to bed.

'But it turned out that everyone who was attacked had been fishing. No one really knows – perhaps there was enough scent of fish on them, perhaps they had wiped their pants or still had the scent on their hands – but that was the only link we could think of. If the sow was really hungry and her cubs were too, perhaps that is what got her brave enough to attack the first tent and then she found there was something worth coming back for.' A flash of sadness crossed Jan's face. 'Who knows really?'

She caught herself then, realising it was pointless to remind herself of the tragedy, and busied herself clearing plates, leaving me to ponder. I was here to talk to her about wolves but we had become sidetracked by the subject of bears, as so often happened here.

Living with bears is tough and scary. People regularly get attacked if they are in the wrong place at the wrong time or are simply not vigilant enough. Human attacks are increasing as bears increase their numbers and move into more populated areas. Yet – based on evidence of sightings and encounters and the fact that dead sow was found to be underweight, had only eaten vegetarian food, had never touched human food and had parasites in her belly – if it's difficult for us to live with bears, it's certainly more difficult for them, particularly the females.

CHAPTER NINETEEN

I Don't Believe in Signs

The natural world works in funny ways. Of late I had lost completely my faith in signs, serendipity, 'it was meant to be' or any of those things that I had relied upon for years. Cynicism – the result of finding out that the worst-case scenario was actually true most often – had set in.

One morning, awake early, I watched the sky change colour behind the beech tree, slowly revealing its shape as the night's sky turned to grey. Little by little, it showed its branches until finally the sun rose and revealed the trunks were grey-green, the leaves were lime drops, and I could discern the shapes of small birds also waking up.

I knew this beech tree so well. I knew it in every season and at every time of year. I could see it from my bed and my kitchen, from my vegetable garden and my patio. I saw its full orange autumn glory, its naked wintriness, its great spring unfurling, its dense cloak of summer and all the days in between. It was a comfort from the moment we got home, leading me through the seasons as if nothing had changed, although so much had.

I had woken with the subject of love on my mind: whether it was real; what it was; if it had ever existed and, if it had, whether it was forever lost. The brain is still processing stuff even while we sleep and are no longer in charge – fuzzy memories that suddenly make sense, thoughts that shift, ungraspable as they glide from sleeping to waking.

Never mind love and all that bollocks, I got busy – partly to distract myself from 'silly spectral thoughts' and partly because that is what a mum has to do first thing in the morning. Rarely does a teenage boy come downstairs and say, 'I'm not really hungry this morning, some simple fruit will suffice.' At least, not in our house.

In a rush, I headed to the car but I had only taken two steps onto the bridge when I was stopped in my tracks.

There, on the river wall, gleaming right below the beech tree, was a golden heart. Not just a small one either – this heart took up most of the height of the wall, the river flowed beneath it and it was impossible to ignore. I looked around me, sure there must be some explanation, something the sun's rays were reflecting from. Not to say there wasn't anything but, for the life of me, I couldn't see it. Like the tree that grew above it, I had seen that wall below the beech tree in every season, in every light, in every type of morning, but not once had I seen this and it was utterly beautiful.

I took it in. This was a clear sign . . . wasn't it? Of love? At the very least, hope that it might exist. And I couldn't deny that the golden light seemed to touch a place, close to my ribcage, that had been numb for a very long time.

CHAPTER TWENTY

Creation

I used to collect stone hearts, finding them everywhere I walked. I remember the one I found near Kelly, in Wyoming, and another memory comes back of a different kind of wild woman.

Teton Science School is not where you would expect to find an art studio, but here – under a log cabin, down some wooden stairs – is just that, and it's a magical place where everyone is welcome. It's not your usual art studio or gallery; this is a place full of treasures, art that you want to touch, hug and hold, and where a river made of woven fabrics with felted rocks and rapids meanders across the floor.

The artist-in-residence is Doris Florig, who spends her summers in Jackson Hole and winters elsewhere (as many of the population of Jackson Hole do when their bones start to complain about the long, harsh season but their heart isn't ready to leave). Doris is a fibre artist. The walls are hung with the tapestries she weaves, and I am surrounded by sculptures. Wilderness is her inspiration.

'On the way here, I pass the bison,' she tells me, referring to the herd of bison that hang out and overwinter in the Kelly area just north of town. You can usually see them from the road, and if you are in a hurry you can guarantee one or a few of them will be blocking the road, ambling across. 'The other day I passed maybe four hundred bison. And I sat there and just looked at them. I spent an hour, hour and a half watching 'em, trying to figure out where they go and what they do. And I'm always trying to figure out where they've been.'

As someone who is interested in wild animals, this is something I can relate to, but the next thing she says is off at a slight tangent for my brain: 'Because I like to collect bison hair.'

'You like to collect the hair?' I look at the studio around me – of course she does.

'But I don't dare get out of the car when they're around. I wait and look for it when the bison are gone.'

Well, it's not as bad as giving them a good brush and seeing what comes off them. Many of the tourists who visit are in the dark about these goofy-looking amblers. The bison can actually be quite dangerous if they feel threatened, and those small, cute horns on top of their dim-looking faces have been known to gore people through and kill them.

Doris's work isn't just about observing the bison or the natural world around her; she really immerses herself in it, but not in a predictable way – like the swimming or hiking, wildlife-spotting or exploring that I like to do. Doris is all about using the resources to make art.

'I make these sculptures out of fibre. I'm working on a lynx, I'm working on a mountain goat, and everything I do I like to work full-size. So that's why you are surrounded by all these life-size pieces. I'm working on this bison head – I've already done several of them, I just love them. I think of it a bit like the hunters who go out and get their trophy and it's a bison's head that they want to stick on their wall. Well, I offer something very different because conservationists are not going to have a trophy in their house, but they can have one of my mounts. It's full size and it kind of fools people at first. They walk in and think *hmm, does this person really have a bison head in here?*

'The best part about doing the bison is that I go out and collect my own fibres. I watch the bison to see where they are and then I don't get out of the car, I wait until the next day. I come back and check the areas where they walked through. Not these trees so much,' she waves at the giant aspens around us, 'but the evergreen trees. As they walk through, especially in the spring, they rub up against the trees and there'll be little tiny fibres of bison hair. It's not much. When I go out collecting I could collect for fifteen

minutes and come back with just a handful of bison hair.
But it's pretty exciting to go out and it's like being on a
treasure hunt, finding these little fibres and collecting them,
and before you know it you have a handful.

'Like I said, each day on the way here, I pass the bison.
In the spring I see them and then, all of a sudden one day,
all the females come out with their calves. Their calves are
like cinnamon. Just beautiful. Then the next day I watched
I could see that they were kind of in packs. The females
had their calves right beside them, and the guys that were
born the year before – the teenagers – were off and had
created their own pack so I think they were being forced
away. And then it was mating season, maybe three weeks
ago, and each time I came through there would be more
and more; the herds were converging. Usually the males
are not with the herd but now they were converging, and I
noticed lots of motion, movement.

'Just following them from season to season is really
incredible. I see so much, and I just sit there and watch
them, or creep along in my van and see where they're going.
Try and figure out where they're coming from, where
they're going. Then I also feel like I'm even getting to know
them. The day I was watching those four hundred bison and
trying to pick out the leader, I thought *hmm, I wonder if I
recognise any of these guys?* You start to know them individually.'

She shows me a piece she is currently working on that is
inspired by the aspen trees shimmering all around the
collection of log cabins here. Aspens change so much
through the seasons, and in each they are beautiful – in my
time in Wyoming I came to love them as much as our UK
trees – and Doris's vision seems to be to capture all the
seasons of the aspens in her fabric forest. But she doesn't do
it the easy way.

'This aspen tree, the next one I do,' she says, 'I want to
make it a fall foliage tree. So I'm gonna go out and collect
aspen leaves and I'll put them in a pot and simmer it like I'm

making tea. And then, after it brews, I take that out and I put
the fibres in the water, and then pull it out and I think I'm
gonna come up with a really nice yellow.'

'You don't know?'

'I'm experimenting all the time; you don't always know.
Then I'll cut that coloured wool fabric into the shape of the
aspen leaves and then mount it onto my trees.'

It must take ages. Although the trees are not quite full
size, they fill the room from floor to ceiling, as do the
tapestries and a giant loom. There is so much to take in that
I'm just gazing around at it all, but Doris sees where I am
looking.

'The tapestries? Tapestries are really exciting because this
is something that's been done since the 1400s, 1500s. They're
nice because people are drawn to them. They're all made of
wool, all natural fibres, and people connect – perhaps
because our clothing is fibres. So when people see my
tapestries it really warms them up. And tapestries are different
from paintings because tapestries absorb the light. When
you look at a painting it's reflecting the light, but when you
look at a tapestry it's absorbing the light and gives a feeling
of warmth. And the other nice thing is that it's great for
acoustics.'

I have to admit there is a cosiness in this room that I
haven't experienced in any other art studio, even though
every depiction – from tapestry to sculpture to the river on
the floor – is designed to remind us of what is outside in the
often harsh natural world.

'Can I touch it?'

'Of course you can.'

I find myself stroking the bison head and fighting the
urge to sit on a rock under the aspen.

'Why is the natural world so important to you?' I ask
Doris.

'I just connect to it all the time. I'm just looking constantly
and figuring out . . . you know, what colour is this tree? And

how can I get these shapes? It forces me to look more closely at things, and it forces me to learn new techniques in order to get new shapes.'

I ask what Doris thinks the power of this landscape is, and why it attracts us.

'Well, it's just totally amazing,' she says. 'Everywhere you look, the change is constant. Every time you turn around, the lighting is different. It's unbelievable. Being out here at the Teton Science School, there's wildlife around all the time. Every now and then I'll ride my bike – to get a break, get out of my studio and go outside – and last fall I was on my bike and I heard this noise and thought *hmm, what is that?* I could hear this crashing around in the woods and I looked up and, the next thing I knew, a moose came down the hill. She ran this side of me, and then the bull moose came on this side of me. It was rutting season and I thought *oh, this is not good*, but it all happened so fast. I just stood there, and he chased her – they weren't interested in me. But then a young moose came down the hill and he stopped. He was looking and looking, so I took my bicycle and just swung it around and stood with it in front of me, hoping that if he got any closer I'd have some kind of protection. But he looked a little while and then he took off.'

Doris laughs at the memory and I understand – that feeling that you were just lucky enough to witness something special in the natural world but also that you were at risk by doing it. I had experienced that 'oh, this is not good' moment on a couple of occasions myself, as have most people I know who like the natural world.

'When I think of wilderness,' she says, 'I like to think of things that are untouched. And I think these surroundings, in the Tetons, are amazing. The number of people these parks handle, and still things are left untouched. And I think it teaches people when they come through the park that they don't have to take something home with them. That what they're taking home is something new and different here. It's experience.'

I ask Doris what her art does – whether she thinks it gives people a greater appreciation of nature, and whether she feels it's like a vocation. She is almost reluctant to reply, but finally she says quietly: 'Yeah. I think what my art does is that, maybe, it helps people connect to nature.'

I ask why that connection to nature is important, and what she gets from it. She is thoughtful now, as if I'm asking how she takes a breath or how she digests her food.

'Well, my connection to nature forces me to see my surroundings. If I weren't doing art, I might be just driving along and not noticing things. But now I'm constantly looking, I'm looking at the colour of the tree, I'm looking at the shapes. And it has taught me that it's important for me to learn more about science. I think it's important that people realise that science and art are connected.

'An example is if I'm working on one aspen tree to the next, I'll see a different aspen tree. But before I started doing this, I would have looked at an aspen tree and just said, *oh, this one has spots*. I never would have thought, *wow, there was a branch growing out of there! That's why that spot's there.* Then sometimes you see other markings and go, *oh, now I understand!* You see, the elk love to hang out in the aspens because it's a moist area and it's a very comfortable area. And if they need to in the winter, they'll eat the bark from the tree. So if you look closely, you'll see areas where the elk have been eating the bark.'

'So there's always a scientific explanation for what comes to you as a beautiful pattern or a beautiful thing?'

'Yes. Exactly that.'

'So what arises from this simple scientific fact is beauty?'

'Yes. So then,' she pauses to think, 'something scientific that happens – like the elk taking a chunk off or a branch growing and then dropping off – it all makes the textures and patterns.'

'And leaves you with something beautiful.'

'Yeah!'

I can tell from her smile that Doris is excited that I'm coming to an understanding. So many people come here to this studio to learn and talk, and it's clear that her art is about sharing.

'It's probably the same as people: when they go out in the winter, to track animals and look at the footprints – just by seeing those things they create the story. I started researching and learning more and more about science. When I was growing up, science was just a subject I took in school. Now it's something that's really important to me, and I spend a lot of time in the library here, I spend a lot of time talking to the scientists around here, I'm always picking their brains. I'm wanting more information because that information affects the way my work comes out.'

'For you, then,' I say, 'there is an intimate relationship between science and art.'

'Yeah, I see it more and more all the time – the relationship between science and art.'

Outside, a light rain has begun to fall as I wander through the real aspens back to my car. I feel at peace, calm and happy, having spent an hour cross-legged on the floor, making felted river rocks to add to the river bed and chit-chatting with Doris about wildlife and children while making stuff just for fun.

'What size should I make it?' I had asked. 'What kind of shape?'

'Whatever you feel,' she had replied, 'just see what it turns into.'

Doris's wild world felt remarkably limitless and comforting, despite its bedrock of science. And if there was ever a tree I did want to hug, it was one of hers.

CHAPTER TWENTY-ONE

From Stick to Chick

The one thing a house by a river really needs, if there is space and you are even slightly romantic, is a weeping willow. Arching and elegant, reminiscent of Ratty and Mole and all their adventures, it seemed improbable that there wasn't one here when we arrived.

When Fred was a baby on my back, one of my favourite things do with him was walk up through the fields alongside the river, chatting nonsense about the plants and birds if he was awake, pointing at the cows and throwing a stick for the dogs. We'd usually make it as far as our friends' house, our nearest neighbours upriver, and have a cup of tea and a wander around their garden. On one of these visits, in Fred's first spring, I was so full of admiration for the new green leaves on the trailing branches of the weeping willows there that I snipped off a few twigs and brought them home, just on the off chance.

My gardening style is, at best, 'survival of the fittest'; that much has probably been established. Assuming that river water would be best for their sprouting, and knowing willow spreads readily and loves having its feet wet, I shoved the cuttings into the mud in the stream just by the bridge and left them there. It seemed like a safe bet because I wouldn't need to worry when I forgot to water them.

It wasn't long before extra leaves were appearing and they were getting stronger. A couple of months later, curious, I pulled them out of the mud and found that one had started to grow roots. I planted it on the other side of the river, in full view of the house that very first summer we were here. In no time at all, it was more than a stick and rapidly grew into a young tree with beautiful bowing branches.

Every day I watched it grow without watching it grow. It just lived alongside us, growing in the same way a child grows – in fits and starts that you don't really notice until you look at an old photo or suddenly realise it is taller than you . . . then taller than the fence, then hiding the gate, then spreading leafy branches over the lawn. Eventually I realised that it had become all grown up – as tall as the oldest oak – and that what was once a twig with a few leaves on it was now majestic.

In spring the leaves of the willow as they unfurl are the newest of greens; in the mornings, with the sunlight behind the tree and a slip of mist rising from the river in the new warmth, they begin to glow. The willow had become a nesting spot for a green woodpecker pair. They nested high up and deep in the fork of the branches, so deep that it was impossible to see the actual nest itself, but one morning I couldn't help but notice their constant coming and going. After the classic woodpecker swooping flight across the lawn and up into the branches, they would just disappear. As the leaves grew thicker and fuller on the branches, it became hard to see the woodpeckers at all . . . until one day in early May I was walking across the lawn and noticed a small head poking out from the fork – a little speckled baby woodpecker head, popping out of the hidden nest for a look around. I realised it was actually looking at its sibling, an equally small and spotty but obviously braver chick who had wandered out of the nest and along one of the broad branches. I got the distinct impression this wasn't something that would be attempted by the chick still in the nest and that, in fact, such a brazen act of independence – or fledging – was anxiety-inducing for the more tentative chick, who promptly popped his head right back down with clearly no intention of going anywhere.

I moved further away and kept an eye on things from a distance as the bolder young chick began his life adventure in the new spring sunshine. He spent the day on the branch and was still there as it turned dark. The next morning, one minute he was there and the next he was gone. And later that day I realised there was no other head popping up and peering out of the nest, and no low swooping flights under the arched branches either. I smiled; both had fledged.

SUMMER

CHAPTER TWENTY-TWO

This Place is Buzzing

The flood meadow is awash. Yellow buttercups have transformed it into a work of art through which the dog bounds and I walk. It is impossible not to smile. Flowers are popping up everywhere – not just yellow but purples and blues – tiny flowers that I have to crouch down to inspect, and tall lacy white blooms that look suspiciously like hogweed so I don't get too close. I see the cones of great burnet, soft white clouds of meadowsweet, red clover, oxeye daisies, knapweed, little delicate cuckooflowers like cotton skirts, and other flowers that I have no idea about but that poke through the tangled foliage in a crazy tapestry more beautiful than any human (even Doris) could ever design and that makes my heart sing.

The whole place is buzzing – not like a nightclub, but a better buzz with insects dancing a dance that we need. The evening is warm, even the ground is warm beneath my bare feet now, and butterflies are still working their magic here and there, blue and white, never staying still long enough for me to take a photo. Swifts fly overhead and soon the pipistrelle bats will leave their roost in their hundreds. A glossy yellow-shelled snail works its way up a stem laden with white flowers I don't even recognise, and the spiral pattern it carries looks as though it has been painted by an artist.

I walk the mown paths as slowly as I can. A mini adventure into a wilderness.

Our old plan to save the flood meadow for the species that should be here is working. For everything in life and the world that is going wrong, now – slowly and with a bit of help from me – this little patch is going right and this is its moment. It is a moment to relish because, for all its beauty, I know it won't last long. Time marches on, I know to grab the moment, for a season this is my evening routine and I will treasure it.

CHAPTER TWENTY-THREE

Out of the Depths

I swim in the river most days now the summer has arrived. The fact that it is still deeply cold is merely a battle of the mind, I tell myself, and so it proves to be.

There are enormous health benefits to immersing yourself in cold water and going for a 'wild swim' in the sea or the river. It boosts your dopamine and endorphins and it gets you exercised, so I know I am doing something good for myself, but there is more to it than that.

I don't care what you say, there is no easy way to get in. I'm also reluctant to dive in because there is a sewage works and several farms upstream, so I'd rather keep the whole nostril and mouth area above the water, just in case. It's crazy what we do to our freshwater but that is the reality of life here in the UK. While our rivers are the lifeblood of the countryside, providing highways for all sorts of wildlife from insects to otters, and while we glorify these peaceful places and delight in them, we are also pouring raw sewage into them. Classic.

As I glide up and down the old millpond, I'm accustomed to the temperature and so, other than sewage, I don't really have anything to worry about. I have the odd freak-out about eels, which have been spotted in the river, but I convince myself that they will steer clear of this odd-shaped fish. I enhance my river-nymph look by wearing 'protective footwear' at all times because of the invasion of the signal crayfish. When we first arrived on the river over twenty years ago, there were no crayfish; now when the water goes low, you see armies of them marching down the banks, emerging from holes, massive ones positively stomping and tiny ones writhing in the mud. They are an invasive species that we really don't want in our rivers, but we seem helpless to do much about it. They eat into walls, causing untold damage up and down the country, as well as anything else they can get their powerful pincers on – including some of our native species. I have no intention of having one grasping at my toes and clinging on for dear life while I am taking a serene wild dip.

Once in, there is something utterly soothing about swimming in the river. If there is a time I feel immersed in nature, it is truly when swimming in a wild place. The water is soft and holds me as I move through it, feeling the warmer patches in the sunshine. Dragonflies dart around, birds fly overhead, the river's surface sparkles, and all I hear is the water and birds. I see the whole place from a different angle and the struggle to get in shifts, and now the struggle is to even think of getting out because it is just so beautiful. Whether here in the millpond or further up under the arching trees, this is a moment in the day when, with every sense occupied, I can have a mini adventure and forget all the other stuff. I come out of the water refreshed in a million ways, soothed and yet buzzing at the same time – as if I have had a good brain wash. It brings me a sneaky bit of joy. So I have something in common with a woman I am excited to meet online. Yet, at the same time, we have nothing in common because here in my quaint little English river there is no such thing as a great white shark, and where she goes wild swimming there most definitely is.

———

Pippa Ehrlich is co-director of the award-winning and phenomenally popular Netflix film *My Octopus Teacher*. It's the ultimate wild-swimming story, resulting in an extraordinary 'relationship'. Underwater cameraman Craig Foster makes friends with an octopus while freediving in the kelp sea forest off Cape Town in South Africa, a place known for its population of great whites. On the day we chat, Pippa is cautiously pushing down bewildered excitement as they have been told they may be about to receive an Oscar nomination (which turned into an actual nomination and then an actual Oscar). I am in lockdown, and so is she with the South African sun shining brightly outside the window behind her.

Pippa understands the challenges of the wilderness only too well, working in the cold seas off South Africa was no joke, and the subject of their film was essentially a fast-moving snail without its shell. Yet, despite the challenges, the team managed to create a film in which there is intimacy and connection and, above all, one in which we care deeply about the main character – a phenomenal feat when the octopus species is so unlike us. Along the way, we also learn a lot about a life and a wild place other than our own.

Pippa tells me that the training was tough. Hers was not a lazy dip before lunch. Just to get into the right physical and mental shape to make the film – to be present for long enough under the water to capture something meaningful – meant going way out of her comfort zone.

'Animals, particularly underwater, are hard to predict so you can't always plan your story and you have to work hard to get close to them,' she says. 'Working in the ocean means there are so many other factors to consider: the swell direction, the wind direction, the clarity of the water, affecting how far you can see and what you can film, and of course when and where you are safe.'

The place where they were filming, off the South African peninsula, is known as the Cape of Storms. It shows nature's forces at their most powerful and it is a place to be respected.

'In our case it was more crazy. We wanted to feel closer to nature, with no barriers, so we decided to work without wetsuits. I had to adapt my body to the cold water (temperatures are as low as 7°C), which took six months. A small part of us is still governed by instinct and evolution, but I went swimming every single day before or after work. I started with just twenty minutes until, in the end, I broke through and I could stay in for an hour. Craig was amazing and he did more than that – he could sometimes last for two hours. There were lots of times when I just didn't want to go but, once you are in and once you have done it, it feels so good.'

Pippa and I talk a little about how the wilderness and natural world challenge us in that way, especially when we are working within it. I'm intrigued about its very tough boundaries and the way we can overcome them, and Pippa's feeling is that much of it is simply in our own minds.

'Once I got over the barriers in my own head, that was when I was able to stay in for longer and I made that leap from twenty minutes to an hour. Once you stop resisting something, you can surrender to it. We all have the ability to do that. Once you expose yourself to some primal fear you have, suddenly your meaning is restored.'

I agree: fear, it seems, is what keeps most of us disconnected, at different levels from the natural world. It is undoubtedly a useful instinct, but I often wonder if keeping ourselves safe and comfortable comes at the expense of a connection that we really need on some biological level. Perhaps that is why natural history films are so popular: viewers get all the connection with none of the hard work or risk. And the underwater world off South Africa is a particularly risky place to witness.

'It's a wilderness we feel disconnected from because it seems scary and hard to get to,' says Pippa. 'When you are there, you realise that it is actually similar to our world on the surface; the kelp forest is like a land forest, schools of fish are like flocks of birds. The aim of the film was to transport you to another magical world, to experience that place under the surface.'

Much of that is true but, for me, it's really that strong connection with the octopus that makes the film so successful and such a wonderful surprise to watch.

'In any story,' Pippa says, 'you need a character to relate to and care about. Most of an octopus life is lived in tension and fear. If you think about it from an evolutionary point of view, a snail that lost its shell makes it soft and vulnerable, so that means they need strategies to deal with that. In the filming we saw that they are super-smart learning machines but they also have lots of amazing adaptations, which have occurred over so much time – they have had over 200 million years on the planet. It's so weird to think that 400 million years ago we were both just a wormlike thing.'

The octopus is about as 'science fiction' as a creature can get. There is even a theory that suggests a meteor with alien viruses crashed down to Earth, infecting squid and turning them into octopuses. I guess it's a way of making sense of their mystery, their 'otherness'. I mean, their shape is the first thing that seems so utterly strange to us, and the fact that they have no bones. How does that work? And what does that feel like? And then to have all those 'legs'? They can change colour and even pattern instantly to match their background, they can change shape, they can use Newton's third law to warp to super-speed as if they have jet propulsion. They can squirt ink, and if they lose a limb they can even grow it back. They are a cephalopod, so they are more closely related to a snail than to a human, and yet we see so much that we can relate to in this story of a life lived underwater.

'An octopus is so different from us,' says Pippa, 'yet it has a personality and can communicate. An octopus looks back at you and holds your gaze and yet it is a snail – a snail we can relate to. Octopuses are amazing: they recognise individuals in aquariums, and they can hate people and can squirt water at them depending on their past experience with them. They clearly have a desire to connect with humans too, and the idea comes across in the filming that she is actually feeling something too, especially in the hunting-the-crab story.'

This story in the film comes not long after the octopus has grown back the leg that she lost in a shark attack.

Recovered, she is back to hunting normally and Craig is getting ever closer to her life. She spots a crab while Craig is with her, and he describes how the crab hides underneath an anemone. The octopus then waits and hides, patient until the crab thinks everything is OK and comes out from under the anemone. The crab makes a dash for the kelp and then lands happily on the sea bed, seemingly oblivious to the fact that he is being watched and stalked by a master of disguise . . . until the very last second, when his final attempt to 'sprint' away is unsuccessful and he is devoured by the octopus. As she is eating, she is overwhelmed by brittle stars (a kind of starfish) that try to steal her food. In response, she changes her behaviour. Craig describes how she goes and hides in a den with her food and simply throws the brittle stars away every time they come in. Lobsters are not as easy as crabs; she struggles to catch them until she figures out how to use Craig as part of her strategy and gets close enough, using him as a barrier, to throw herself over the top of the lobster so they can't escape. We constantly see her learn new ways of doing things.

'Science is the most important thing to happen in our world,' Pippa says, 'and yet science is sometimes so limiting. The world is in trouble right now; we can't afford to keep telling stories in a way that makes them numb or over-rational. As a scientist, I was excited to tell a story that made people care through their heart not their head.'

The surprise discovery of the octopus, right on Craig's doorstep, was the perfect character to do just that.

'Craig filmed lots of behaviour that surprised science, like armouring – a brand-new "transformer technique", where the octopus defends herself by using the suckers on her tentacles to quickly pick up shells or pebbles and turn them into a protective cover, like a shield. She also weaves a basket of kelp leaves around herself. We wouldn't see that in captivity because there are no predators. We even had a scientist fly in; Dr Jennifer Mather studies human and cephalopod behaviour. She flew from America to watch hours of our footage. She is difficult to impress, but even she was blown away. We've come into a golden age of nature filmmaking and all the obvious stories have been seen and shared. Now you have to work carefully with scientists and rely on them to share things that you never imagined.'

I ask her about the Oscar nomination and, although they are thrilled, Pippa sees a much bigger picture: 'Never do anything for the honour or the glory,' she says, 'or your world will only go weird.' It is something I see often in the business of people who work in conservation or with wild animals – that concept of a bigger picture, something bigger than our own egos to work for, or the knowledge that nature is a great leveller but also needs our care. So the Sea Change project was built by the team who produced the film – a way to use this understanding of the underwater world to connect people with it and motivate them to protect it – a cause for a greater good.

As much as *My Octopus Teacher* is a film about an octopus and her life, it is also a film about healing. Craig is very honest about having burn-out at the start of the film, and that he turned to the ocean to feel better and recover so that he could be a better father after his marriage failed. In my own exploration, I have also come up against the healing power of the wilderness, of nature, of mystery as well as questions that – for all our technology and intelligence – we have yet to find the answers to, like whether an octopus can also feel joy.

CHAPTER TWENTY-FOUR

An Enduring Theme

There was no doubt about it any more. No time to question and no point to asking why, although the general consensus was fungus. The willow was dying.

I had noticed it, but been afraid to acknowledge it. The river had been low, the weather reports had been bemoaning our lack of rainfall, and so I had used that to justify the increasing fragility and lack of leaves on the willow branches. But slowly the leaves that were left had shrivelled and fallen. There was no point in me watering it. No point in praying for it. The life in it was simply gone and was past the point that anything I could do would bring it back.

The time where every day I loved the sheer miracle of it, the years of watching it grow – that time was over. Before the autumn winds came, it would be best to cut it down. It was like saying goodbye to a silent friend.

It took no time at all to come down. Rotten inside, it had been the right decision.

Witnessing a tree go from a stick to a beautiful presence taller than the house, become home for birds, a shady spot on the lawn, and the perfect neighbour for the river meant I had assumed that it would be there for ever, part of the landscape. And yet it was done.

The tree that I had planted with Fred as a baby beside me was now ending its life, while Fred was now taller than me and beginning his.

The space it left seemed enormous. But perhaps I could save a cutting and hope for a new life.

CHAPTER TWENTY-FIVE

Acceptance

To enter the house and garden of Jonathan and Angie Scott is to enter an atmosphere of deep peace and tranquillity after the colour and the chaos of Nairobi's streets. I'm here for lunch, following a week's work in Nairobi, and their relaxed charm wraps me like a longed-for cashmere blanket. The light here is golden and pure, warm and balmy.

I've known Jonathan and Angie for many years. For Angie, photographing wildlife is her lifelong passion. Jonathan, likewise. The two artists and devoted conservationists are the only couple to have won the Wildlife Photographer of the Year as individuals – Jonathan in 1987 and Angie in 2002. They remain not only distinctive in what they each do, but together they also create something even more magnificent. They married in Kenya's Maasai Mara game reserve in 1992 and they just fit. It's hard to describe the feeling that flows between them, but it is gentle and respectful, loving and kind.

Angie is all kind of zen, with captivating long blonde hair, and she is lean and ethereal somehow. But I'm not going to get carried away because Angie is actually very rock and roll, and probably an OG when it comes to wild women – a subject that our conversation drifts to effortlessly.

'A lot of the women that I know that are doing extraordinary work in the field, they *have* to do it. It's sort of a burning-up for them to be in the field and do what they do, and they can't get distracted by relationships and all that that brings to the party.'

She talks with her hands constantly, her long fingers never stopping moving, weaving together and apart.

'I am a visual person so I don't think with words so much. You have to be incredibly mindful and very quiet and a very good listener. You are listening to what you are seeing, if that makes sense. There is a sort of "beyond the veil", where you are quiet and you sort of slip into that other world. The words shuffle off here and you sort of absorb the essence of what you are seeing. That can come out in the imagery. I always think that imagery is far more powerful than words. For us, we are very lucky because Jonny can write the story and I can illustrate but I find talking about things is quite hard. After being with the lions for days and days – just me and the pride – I wish that I could share what I am witnessing, this extraordinary bond they have that is almost beyond understanding, beyond language. They are just a sisterhood; they fill in the gaps. They are a sisterhood in that they are constantly reaffirming their place in this pride, which makes them so strong, and it is a miracle to watch. I have learned so much about the bonding of females and how it makes us stronger. We should be in unity together because then we are very, very powerful. We shouldn't be doing what I see a lot of the younger generation doing, which is scrabbling and grasping for power. We don't need power, we need just to be ourselves.

'I think it helps to have a lineage of very strong women too. I had a very extraordinary grandmother, for instance, who I watched avidly while I was growing up. She was, especially, the epitome of an extraordinary horsewoman. My great-grandparents lived in Alexandria in Egypt, which was where I was born. They were very connected to the Greek community and were very bohemian – artists and writers. My grandmother was scooped up by a very handsome cavalry officer and she just went off to South America at the beginning of the century and travelled on mule back up into the mountains of Argentina, to Córdoba. He wrote a book and he was a painter, he captained the Argentine polo team, spied for Britain in both World Wars and rode with Lawrence of Arabia, while she was incredibly spiritual. She arrived right up in these mountains and he would disappear for months at a time and leave her, and the stories of how she brought up my mother and my uncle there alone are amazing.

'My grandmother had always been this figure that I looked up to far more than my mother, because she would ride as well as the men. You know, she was left alone to deal with the whole farm and the horses and everything as well as the men. I mean, we complain when our men disappear on work trips but seriously?! My grandfather was tall, dark, handsome, wild, and she was very elegant, beautiful and lovely as well as running this whole place in the middle of nowhere. I think having people like that in your life that you admire and look up to makes a huge difference.

'My childhood also made me who I am. When I was four we moved to Dar es Salaam in Tanzania and obviously at the time there was no internet – in fact, there was no anything like that – but it was an amazing childhood. All we had was the outdoors. There was me and my brother and we were so close. He was older so he would make me do all sorts of adventurous things that little girls probably shouldn't do and, because I hero-worshipped him, I did everything. So we would disappear outside all the time. We had little boats we would sail out to the islands, we would sleep under the stars, and there was never that thing from the parents of, "Oh my goodness, where are they?" We just weren't there.'

We both laugh, acknowledging just how unusual that would be now.

'We were really little, you know? The background of childhood for me was always the Serengeti or going up into the mountains. It really was a childhood of paradise.

'I met the first man to kayak around South Georgia, Graham Charles, when we were in Antarctica and he said the importance of getting children out into the natural world when they are really little is so that they aren't frightened of it. Instead it cocoons them and it supports them, so any time they are in trouble they can go for a walk or sit under a tree and understand the power that nature pulls. He also ran this programme for children to assess any danger and then deal with it. We didn't have that when I grew up, we were just free to do anything and everything we felt like doing – riding horses off into the bush or whatever – but it would empower young people and their parents to be able to assess risk, to know the difference between acceptable risk and foolhardiness, and how to deal with things when they went awry.

'It probably helped that my parents had grown up like that too. My father grew up in South Africa and my mother in Argentina, so they had that confidence that it was OK to sleep under the stars and you didn't have to be tucked up in bed at night. That is how I brought my children up too.'

'Do you think that childhood freedom informs what you give yourself permission to be as a woman?' I ask, slightly shocked by my own question.

'I think we are beaten down a lot as we grow up. I went from Africa into the European school system and I got into such trouble. I really didn't mean to be in trouble but I was. I would take my shoes off and run down the corridors but it was just because I didn't like shoes. It was the kind of thing that I just didn't think about. It was a very harsh transition because you have to conform. You don't want to be outside the lines, you don't want to be "bad" and it is really hard to see how you can fit. You end up feeling that you never fit really after an upbringing like that. You never fit anywhere because you are a free spirit. You only fit if you are in the Mara with the lions or trekking up a mountain – that is when you are in your zone and your zen place.

'Then it is time to find a relationship where you fit. If you are lucky, you find a man who is able to allow you to be whatever it is that you are with no judgement – making mistakes, climbing a mountain looking a state, falling, tripping, picking yourself up again. I always felt that we women had to look a certain way or be a certain way or conform in a certain way, and that stifles us, but now I think differently. I have a lot of women in my life who I love teaching and I mentor, and a constant theme between them all as they get to a certain age is: "I'm waiting for the right time to have a baby. I've got to be really settled, I've got to have a house and a man and stable finances and a pushchair and a cot and all the right things that my girlfriends have, and then I can have a baby." I see it differently. I don't think you need to conform like that for your child to blossom. I took my daughter off to Australia when she was two and I home-schooled her because it was easier. I don't think it did her any harm; she saw the world. My son too has travelled to most of the countries there are in the world. In every country from India to Japan, we would meet people and get to know people, and the kids loved it. Sometimes we would do simple things like pulling off the side of the road on safari in Kenya and sleep under the stars.'

Both Angie's kids are grown now, with their own lives, but she says, 'I think that more than anything, my son loves even now to always connect back to nature in whatever way he can.'

So, what does this wild woman fill her days with now?

'I have one picture that I am working on at the moment. I have been sitting with one particular pride every day. You just sit and find a little quiet spot a way away, watching this extraordinary dynamic of cubs and mothers and how they interact throughout the day. Then they are sleeping and something else happens and then a hyena will come in . . . You are just witnessing their lives from a distance and absorbing what you are doing. Then four o'clock comes and the [tourist safari] cars charge in.

'Recently, there was one of the older females that had just had cubs and, because of the lack of the vegetation that is happening at the moment due to global warming, elephants, cattle, fire, a lot of the den sites for the lionesses have been demolished. The cars just don't take any notice and crash through the bushes. She put the cubs in this bush, and all the lionesses were taking in the shade around the bush and it was like a little small arena; the bush was in the corner and there was a drop-off into the swamp so she couldn't go that way. I had parked myself in the corner quite a way away, but the cars charge in and go straight up to the bush to see if they can get the tourists a look at these little tiny cubs. The cubs are too little to be brought out. The mother doesn't even want to bring them out to the rest of the pride; she has hidden them. This one particular guide was irritated and started getting the car and pushing into the bush. The lioness who was called Kali picked up one of the cubs and ran towards my car – because it gave her a way to get out – and I have this picture as she comes towards me and her eyes are like saucers with this tiny cub in her mouth.

'Even now it just makes my heart break because she has also had to leave the others. I mean, what are we doing? People have no clue about the trials and tribulations of these lions. They are so extraordinarily tolerant, these lionesses, because they could fight back – they could jump into that car and haul you out and munch you – but they don't. They just want to live their lives in their pride, doing their thing calmly. They are very zen, lionesses. Every day they just get up, bond, lick and share – they share their milk with other cubs if one mother doesn't have enough. They don't deserve human beings just destroying their territory, but that is what we are doing.'

I ask where the males fit in to the pride.

'Like all nature, it works,' says Angie. 'It's harsh but it still works perfectly. Normally you would have two maybe three males in a pride, but they are often off patrolling or resting up together. The females do most of the hunting, the males will come and drive the females off, but will let the smallest cubs eat with them. When they've had enough, they move off and go and find a bush and hang out under there while the females then come in and finish whatever it is they have killed.'

I think back to what Athena said about energetics and the fact that in hunter-gatherer societies it is the women's work that enables the community in terms of calories gathered.

'The males are constantly patrolling the territory to try to make sure other males don't come in,' Angie continues, 'because that is when everything goes awry. There is a benefit to that: when males get old, it is good to have a new gene pool coming through, so the new males come in and they push the old males out and they kill the cubs prompting the females to come into season and breed with them.

'I witnessed that when I was with one of my favourite lionesses. These three new males had been tracking her every move. Her little ones were slightly younger than the rest of the pride so she had taken herself away until they were older, and they tracked her down. She fought tooth and nail to try to protect the cubs – with a lot of aggression – any time they came near she went ballistic. They killed one, they killed two, and they killed three, and then there was one left. I have a whole series of pictures as she faced down this one male to protect her last cub. You would think *why is she bothering, for goodness sake?* But it is that female thing that is so powerful. Eventually the male managed to get the cub, shook it and killed it and left it on the ground. And it was extraordinary because, within an hour or so, she was courting the male and being really friendly, getting ready to mate.

'I was by myself and upset and I came back and said, "OK, just explain this one to me," and Jonathan said, "Ange, the cub is dead, the cycle of life goes on." She has totally accepted it, without all the angst that we humans have when we don't accept something. It just shows how different a lion's reality is from ours. We put so much meaning and emotion and tragedy and drama on everything that happens, we have made life so complicated. We still don't really understand anything about love and humans and human relationships. As dearly as I love my darling husband, we talk and we disagree and I find myself saying, "no, that's not how it is!" We have a different reality; it isn't wrong, that's just the way of life.

'Lions, I think, accept that. They live by their own voices. The males are patrolling and trying to keep the other males away so that the females can do what they do best – which is nurturing the little ones growing up, teaching them how to be a lion, getting the food. There is a natural division of labour and it works. Very occasionally you might get a male that has a different relationship with the cubs and hangs out more with the females; we have had one or two in the past who were so sweet with the cubs. But then what do we know, really? We are meant to be lion experts but as humans we are just making it up; it's just what we perceive as a human, so we are putting our own emotions on the creatures and we might be wrong. Scientists always think they are right but I always query it, I'm not a scientist.'

'Against the backdrop of science, do you think our relationship with the wild as women has often been ignored?' I ask.

'Yes, I think it is has recently. One of my dearest friend's grandmother was a spiritual healer in America. You find a lot of the healers are women who work with herbs. Often their mothers have been herbalists and there is that whole connection with nature. It is another element of our relationship to the wild, which was very prevalent thousands of years ago. When you look at many ancient civilisations, it is often women who were involved in traditional medicine and the healing arts. But when I am with my friend – every time we are together, staying here – we go to meditate by the pool and on each occasion an eagle wheels overhead, calling. It only happens when he is visiting. There is something we are missing in the twenty-first century; there is wisdom out there – we just need to reconnect to it. There is something else, whatever we call it.

'When we met, Jonny was very pure science and I was very pure spiritual. On my side of the bedside table were books on the Dalai Lama and women who walk with the wolves and all that; on Jonny's side was all the scientific hardcore stuff. Now it has completely swapped. I'm now fascinated in physics and quantum physics and all that side of things and how it relates to nature. I don't know enough so I just avidly read. And of course Jonny has been brought into my world and he sees that there is definitely something, there is definitely communication between species and humans. You can't deny it – you only have to have a dog or a cat to know that there is something that we communicate. It's a fascinating world and a fascinating subject and we will never understand – certainly not in my lifetime – how or why. Why do the lions always come and sit by my car? They don't know me as such, they might know my car, but maybe they feel the energy of somebody who is totally quiet, non-threatening, just reading their book. The same with cheetah: are they employing senses that we have lost? You can't quantify it scientifically but when you witness it often enough you know.

'One particular time I was watching over Honey (a cheetah), and her little one and there was nobody else around. I was on a ridge, nobody could see me, high up with a steep drop down to the plains and I was maybe a hundred yards back from the edge. There was one tree and she had made it her own, and I was sitting in the boiling-hot sun all day without even a film crew to film anything if it happened. It was so quiet that you could hear a pin drop, and there wasn't any wind, it was still as anything. Suddenly she gets up as if she has been stung by bees and runs to my car and stands there, staring at the ridge. I'm thinking, *why is she doing that?* And I get my binoculars out and I'm scanning but I can't see anything. I'm thinking, *what am I missing here? There must be something, she is so agitated.* Then she runs in the other direction and I think, *I'm going to sit here until I find out what on earth has spooked her.* The grass was short, and I could see right to the edge of the ridge, so I waited about half an hour and finally a lioness appeared at the top of the ridge and started to follow her. How did Honey know? I just had a feeling that it wasn't just about seeing, but that she *felt* something was amiss. I don't want to jump to conclusions, but it is such a mystery.

'For me there is enough mystery and enough tantalising clues in science for me to feel we probably don't know a huge percentage of what is really going on. I love science, but I always question it. I think there is something beyond the veil and we haven't quite got there. There are too many stories, too many little things that come up. I love trees, for example, and there are all those experiments and new wonderful books coming out about plants and the energy of plants and that they can feel good energy and bad energy. How? But they have done scientific experiments on it and they have quantified that this happens, and I think that opens a whole other wonderful vista and you just want to share it. As we get older, Jonny and I are getting into teaching and the one thing that perhaps we can teach the next generations is just to be aware, appreciating your life in this moment, to notice, to be present, be mindful there is so much going on – so much extraordinary stuff going on in nature. We can't let it go, we are nothing without nature, so you need to be the guardian of your spot and pass knowledge on.'

I ask Angie if she calls herself a tree-hugger, whether she has literally ever been a tree-hugger.

'Of course,' she says. 'I mean, I have trees here and whenever I'm feeling a little low, I'll just go and sit under them. I have days with trees where I will go and hunker down and meditate before the evening comes in. But I know what you are trying to say. I'm not new-age in that way, I've just found that when I sit with trees I tend to calm down. I do feel there is some energy there that for me is very calming and peaceful and I've done this ever since I was little. I had a tree when I was tiny and I still remember it because I could climb into this little tiny bush – when I was little it looked like a tree – and I could go in there and I had fairies in there. Of course they were just seeds floating down but, whenever I was having a hard time and I wanted to get away from people, I would go in there and sit with the "fairies" and for me that was really very comforting.

'Most of us are called "tree-huggers" or "bunny-huggers" as women because people want to put us down, so one learns to be careful about what one says. Women are constantly accused of being tree-huggers, even if they only just acknowledge that there is a mystery. You must admit, though, that we are very attracted to trees subconsciously. When I am in the Mara I always look for a tree for cool, for shade, for protection, because I feel if I have a tree behind me it's like a sentinel. I think there is now enough evidence, we are starting to understand why it is you can go for a walk in the woods and feel better.

'When I was at boarding school in England my brother and I would go to stay with our aunt on the short holidays because we couldn't fly back home but they lived in the countryside with woods and lakes and rivers. I think back on those days and reflect, *what was it that we did to sustain us?* And it was walking and camping in the woods. We did that through our childhood at school and why? Because it made us feel good. We go for a walk in the woods because it calms us down. We weren't thinking about it – and still most of us don't – but it does clear your head every time, so I don't think it is a made-up thing.

'It does make me laugh, that saying "tree-hugger", because it is often meant to be derogatory but I think, *why not?* They are beautiful things. I love leaning against them and being under them – not because I have something about spirits but because I like it there, it feels good. Have we evolved to do that? Is something calling us from our past? Because we were so connected with nature and the natural world, so what happened?

'Thank goodness there are still people connected and still trying to pass on that knowledge, but they are getting fewer and fewer and farther and farther between. When I was seventeen I lived up on Mount Kenya and some of the old people I met there – the healers working with plants – were fascinating, extraordinary. The depth of their knowledge! But would a scientist say that it's not quantifiable and it's just a placebo effect or do they know something I don't know?

'Funnily enough, there is a group here called the tree-huggers – a handful of us wild, weird women who grow herbs and share ideas – and we do feel that there is something that we are missing if we don't make a stand. There is so much benefit in herbs, and we are losing the plants so fast, even in places like Mount Kenya. Animals use the plants for herbs and healing; you see the big cats when they aren't well, eating grass and plants. Daphne Sheldrick [an elephant conservationist] told me that elephants eat moringa pods, which is an immune-boosting plant and so it is possible that they take that when they don't feel so good.

'These days, women are involved in wildlife photography and conservation more and more. When I came into the field, you have no idea about the flack I got. I won the Wildlife Photographer of the Year and one comment I heard from someone who also worked in the same business was: "You know, women are a liability in the bush," and I'm like, "Excuse me, I was changing the tyre on a Land Rover and driving up to Lake Rudolph before you were out of nappies. By myself. What are you talking about?" But that was very much the perception in those days and so a lot of us hid. I certainly hid behind Jonathan; it was safe there. I didn't need fame, I don't want fortune, I'm happy just loving nature and being out there. People say to me, "You are so lucky, you have all of nature around you." And I say, "Bring it to you! You've got a kitchen – buy some pots, pick up some plants and chat to them when you are cooking." There is always something you can do to bring it in.

'Fortunes change, don't they? But nature never changes, it is life itself, always there and always magically doing its own thing. You just need to be who you are – and find the courage to own it.'

CHAPTER TWENTY-SIX

Letting Go

I forgot to harvest the leeks. Of course I did. I was too busy. First-world problems and all that.

I hadn't beaten myself up. I had meant to at least clear them and plant some lettuce instead, but it turns out that the life of a single mother doesn't lend itself to having much spare time. So I hadn't given it too much thought and had just left them alone.

However, being completely disorganised as usual may have turned out to be a good thing as now I didn't need to shop around for the giant alliums I had been dreaming of. Why doesn't everyone let their leeks bolt?

Giant globes of white flowers, four or five feet tall, the leeks were now majestic and dwarfing the scaffold-plank raised bed that was their stage. They were now the superstars of the veggie garden, attracting the attention of any passer-by. Every single time I went past, they were covered in all sorts of pollinating passers-by too, diving in and loving life. What I had considered another brutal reminder of my uselessness actually turned out to be a thing of beauty and usefulness all at once.

So many people, with good-hearted intentions, have used the words 'let go' to me in recent years. I have tried but, when it comes to family and love, it turns out I don't really know how to do that. How comforting to know that I am actually rather good at letting leeks go.

CHAPTER TWENTY-SEVEN

The Killer Menopause

Now is the time, I am told, to focus on my strengths. So, as I sit on the bench in the sunshine, gazing proudly at my leeks, I contemplate that. It had surprised me to hear a friend say, 'What do you mean you can't think of anything you are good at?' when I was wondering how to remake sense of my life.

'Whale watching?' I had said and she actually laughed.

Perhaps it shouldn't have been the first thing to spring to my mind, but it was actually true. On most occasions when I have been out on a cetacean-spotting mission, I have seen them first. It's not a competition, I know, but I think I get so excited that I am constantly scanning the water on hyper alert.

And my mind wanders again.

On numerous trips to Shetland, I had been determined to see orca. They kept appearing and disappearing but we never coincided. One day, all our filming was finished and so, as a family we decided (with some nagging from me) to drive around the coast and see if we could find them. We knew they had been spotted in the last few days as this pod often hunts seals close to the shore, but the chances were also pretty slim as they never stay in one place for long.

Needless to say, after long hours of driving in the car and travelling by ferry up from the mainland to the lovely island of Yell – and trying to ignore the kids bickering between being blown off their feet at every beach and clifftop – we had decided to finally give up and catch the ferry home to the mainland.

'It was always a long shot,' my husband said.

'I know,' I said, 'but the day isn't over yet.'

'You aren't going to see one now.'

I despondently watched the chemical foam form on the surface of my hot chocolate, collected it from the vending machine and made my way back to the table, staggering a little and trying not to let the rocking of the ferry spill the scalding liquid onto my cold fingers. The kids were pushing each other around so I didn't try to sit with them. Instead I placed the hot chocolate on the table.

I looked up out of the window . . . and there it rose.

'Orca,' I said.

It seemed as though everyone on the whole ferry laughed.

'You won't see orca on the Yell ferry' (which was a fair point in those days).

'No! Orca! There!' I insisted.

And there it rose again, a torpedo-black dorsal fin, bigger than I had ever seen, closely followed by another smaller one.

Orca from the Yell ferry.

I had to sit down then, but I smiled all the way home.

———

We spent lots of time in Shetland. We even had a little house there for a time. It is one of my favourite places in the world, and we saw that pod of orca on many more occasions and even watched them hunt below us while we lay on a clifftop. So I have always read about them, always been fascinated by them and the lives they lead and what we still don't know.

Some of the most recent research has been the most fascinating yet. Orca (and a couple of species of beaked whale) are the only other mammals who have a menopause and where the females have a long 'post-reproductive life' essential to the survival of the species. For female orca, reproduction stops somewhere in their forties but they might live until they are a hundred. Like us, they have a peak of fertility in their lives that then declines and stops in the second half of their life.

Far across the seas, on the other side of the US, the Center for Whale Research has been studying the critically endangered Southern Resident orca population for forty years. This amount of long-term data is not only unique but also invaluable. Orca are in decline largely due to a shortage in salmon, which is largely due to us, of course, and the usual problems we have created of overfishing and habitat destruction. The theory is that older females are really important as repositories for information, such as when and where to find salmon. To test this theory, researchers looked at pod movement. Data recorded over decades showed that the older, post-reproductive females are the ones who lead the way, who know how and where to find salmon even through different years and seasons as salmon availability fluctuates. The ecological knowledge these older females have accumulated is vital to the group and may be one of the factors that has led to their evolution of the menopause as an advantage.[1] (I'm guessing that in the cold ocean there isn't so much of a bother with night sweats or hot flushes.)

In an orca family, sometimes neither sons nor daughters leave their family of origin. This is really unusual in the animal kingdom and it means that, as a female killer whale ages, a greater percentage of her family consists of her children, her genes. Investing in the family as a whole unit supports the reproduction of her genes. When a female reproduces, the calf stays with the family so the group carries the cost of rearing that calf; when a male reproduces, his calf stays with its mother in her family unit, so his family doesn't bear the cost of rearing it. The upshot of this is that the mother can transfer more genetic material through sons without creating conflict or further testing the family group.

It is a matriarchal group, in that it is led by the matriarch. Researchers have observed that sons are more likely to die when their mothers die and that if a mother is in the lead her sons will spend more time following than daughters. Plus, the huge amount of knowledge-sharing required for a young orca to survive can be done by that older orca with younger members of the group. So the effects of the older female who no longer has to invest in reproducing herself are hugely beneficial, if not critical, to orca populations increasing the survival rate of their own offspring and of their offspring's offspring too.[2]

I've always assumed that human women ended up with the menopause because they weren't wild. That is to say, that now we are domesticated with nice warm houses and all the sabre-tooth tigers are gone and there is an Aldi down the road, we just glide too far into old age. Our bodies hadn't expected to do that – they never had an evolution plan much beyond reproducing and so didn't bother evolving a half-decent menopause either. So the menopause was basically the beginning of the end. I crashed into mine in my mid-thirties and had no idea what was going on, only that I felt awful *all* the time. And this is why I make no apology for talking about it – because if people had been talking about it a lot, I might have realised what was going on.

Years later, a doctor was to laugh at my blood-test results and say, 'I don't even know how you are operating on a day-to-day basis. It's extraordinary really. I mean, you actually have *no* hormones, and even in menopause you are meant to have *some*. I've only ever seen one person with hormones this low.' At that point I hadn't really been operating that well on a day-to-day basis – hence the blood tests – and I was a little too miserable to laugh along. Anyhow, it was a bit of a shock to realise that the end was now nigh, that my body was done and packing up shop. Only it wasn't. A little oestrogen here, a little of the right kind of progesterone there, a splash of testosterone (and sadly having to cut out the wine, which didn't really combine well with the whole menopause thing), and all those sleepless nights and brain fog were gone.

Menopause seems, for a woman, like a pretty mean trick. Some men feel that too, I suspect, because so many of them start shifting uncomfortably at the very mention of it

– particularly at the thought that a once-lovely woman might go through the 'big change' and end up a chin-haired hag. Is this the point where that wild woman archetype really comes into play? Is she going to be scary? (Stay calm now, and read on.) After having gone through monthly ups and downs hormonally and then – if we are lucky – pregnancy, birth and breastfeeding, it feels like menopause should be the reward at the end. Finally back to being hormone-free – or at least hormone-stable. So it takes a paradigm shift to look at orca and think that we might actually have evolved to do this too. The plan was perhaps there all along evolutionarily, if evolution can ever be seen as a plan.

Science – well, some of it – can back me up on this. There is evidence to suggest, as with orca, that pregnancy and all that was not enough to guarantee a return on our genes – the theory being that, once relieved of the physical burden of reproduction, we too would be freed up to help the rest of the family by gathering food and sharing our hard-won knowledge from years of surviving in the wild. This isn't panning out so well for modern women since the invention of the internet and online deliveries, which makes knowledge of where you used to be able to source the best carrots slightly redundant, but you see my point. Besides, vibrant with hormones plumping up our life force, we still have lots to do other than advise on good food sources.

What about other primates? It doesn't happen for them; they die earlier than us. What about if we were living a more 'natural' life? Observations of contemporary hunter-gatherer societies with no access to modern medical marvels still show that women live into old age, way beyond their reproductive age. Apparently 'vigorous senior women earned more descendants by feeding grandchildren'.[3] Food-sharing and co-operation are some of the ways we humans have thrived. I'm simplifying the science, but basically the contributions of the grandmothers actually increased the rate of birth for their daughters. Grandmothers can provide food for nursing mothers and infants, a task that was previously assumed to have been taken up by men, and big-game hunting, which has been assumed to have been the main type of food provided by the men, is actually somewhat unreliable in terms of regular food. Grandmothers can also help with weaned children.

When I talk with Athena in Arizona about it all, she says, 'There are two really good reasons for it: firstly, the trade-off between the costs of having your own offspring or switching investment from direct reproduction to investing in grandchildren. The other thing that older women can do is invest in social status, and a high social status can lead to improved viability of children or just improved social standing of the group, which leads to enhanced viability of the genes. As humans a lot of our psychological mechanisms are designed to benefit kin. The second reason is that ovulating is actually quite costly in terms of energy; a woman's metabolism is 25 per cent higher during the luteal phase of the cycle. That is pretty energetically expensive and non-trivial from an evolutionary perspective – it means using a lot more calories – so turning that system off is actually beneficial. Also, every time you ovulate, there is a spike in oestrogen and a spike in progesterone and that increases the characteristics of certain cells that can initiate cancer, so the more cycles you have the greater the risk of cancer.'

But surely cancer wasn't around for wild women who were off living the natural life in the natural world, was it? Isn't cancer just a modern disease because of all our pollutants?

'Cancer has been around since the origins of multicellular bodies,' says Athena, and my mind is blown. How did I not know this? 'We are probably at higher risk of it now, but it has always been around. Multicellular bodies mean that cells have to co-operate with each other. In basic terms, cancer cells break the contract and carry on doing their own thing and multiplying on their own. That's why I call it the cheating cell. It has always been around. There is even evidence of cancer in dinosaurs – we see metastases in dinosaur bones.'

In their paper, 'Grandmothering, menopause, and the evolution of human life histories',[4] the authors even suggest that this modern pattern – a long childhood with late development, fertility peaks and a menopause – may not have appeared until 50,000 years ago, when *Homo sapiens* began to ride high on 'unprecedented ecological and competitive success'. This upsurge in population – this extraordinary evolutionary shoot-for-the-stars that our species made – may even have been *because* of the menopause, not despite it. In other words, 'they had what other, earlier hominids lacked; long postmenopausal lifespans and the associated population dynamics underwritten by grandmothers.' Scientific fighting talk for nans everywhere.

Given the fact that the menopause probably didn't evolve in our lineage until the dawn of *sapiens* (judging from the evidence above), it must have evolved independently in orca because our lines of evolution had long since separated. And it seems it may have evolved in two different species for much the same reasons. I think back to my orca encounters, and those families in the sea, with new wonder.

I reconsider a new-found potential usefulness for myself too, which is always nice. I still have a few burning questions, though: if the menopause is so great for us and our species, why is it so bloody awful to go through? Surely there is only so much food-providing you can do when you are up all night sweating? Would oestrogen gel actually stay on a whale, or do they have no need of it? Why haven't we actually evolved to deal with it better? But science doesn't seem to have an answer to any of that.

A State of Awe

I meet Katie Orlinsky when we are assigned to run a workshop together, something I never thought I'd be doing. Decades younger than me, she has more life experience than I had on my little polished fingernail at her age.

She talks fast, smiles all the time and takes a mean photo. Capturing stories with a camera is what she does – for *National Geographic*, *The New York Times* and many others. She walks in the footprints of many men who have done the type of work she has done before her, yet she treads lightly and creates her own footprints. Her latest story, one that she has been working on for two years, is about healing the wilderness but, when we finally get to spend some downtime together and I hear her own story, it turns out that the wilderness healed her.

'I'm born and raised in New York City. I did not grow up going to the outdoors. My dad was a theatre producer – I'm pretty sure he doesn't even own a pair of sneakers – and my mum was an actress and an acting teacher. I was born and raised in Manhattan and I reached photography through taking pictures at protests. Once I was introduced to activism, I saw photos as a way to tell a story to make a difference, and I really focused on social issues, news and politics and that sort of segued into photographing conflict. I worked a lot for *The New York Times* and was doing more international news stories about the Mexican drug war and ended up starting to cover the Middle East and I covered the Arab Spring. It was an incredibly dangerous situation for journalists and I was in an attack where my colleagues were killed.'

Katie is reluctant to recall the details, and in fact she can't; part of her brain has locked away the awful events of the day when she was so close to the colleagues and friends who died in the attack, and much of the week that followed it. It is still too hard for her to talk about, and we don't need to. I know what happened and I know from colleagues of my own the grim reality and cost to the psyche of covering war stories.

'After that,' she says, 'I had PTSD but also became very disillusioned with photography. But it was the only way I had ever really made money, so it wasn't like it was this career that I could leave. There was this part of me that thought, *OK, maybe this is only temporary – don't throw your camera in the river*, but I had days where I was so angry and everything seemed so unfair and I just wanted to throw my camera away and sabotage things. My career had been built around telling these stories that were really hard and dangerous and scary, but I realised I just wasn't emotionally capable of doing that any more because I was very raw and I would be interviewing someone with a sad story. I still wanted to cover US–Mexican migration and those issues – I'm still very passionate about that – but I would try to interview people and if their story was sad, I would just cry and think, *I'm not really capable of doing this any more*.

'So I was very lucky to get this call out of the blue in 2014 for an assignment to photograph a sled dog race in the Alaskan and Canadian wilderness. I had no idea what to expect and it ended up being this really pivotal moment in my career when I realised how interested I was in telling stories about the environment and about climate change. In the process of photographing this race and all the different villages we would visit, all the people would tell me stories about how they were being impacted by climate change, so it was a way to continue being a photojournalist but work in a place that I discovered I really loved – the wilderness.

'I went there and it was so beautiful and I was so amazed. I had never thought I could be in the wilderness – I never felt like it could be a place for me. I had even been to a college that was in Colorado and really for people that loved to be in the wilderness, but there was something very competitive and very masculine about that and I just wasn't drawn to it; it was all about being extreme and a lot of it felt like it was very classist. I mean, I didn't grow up with parents who would take me on these trips, so I didn't have the right clothes for it, and I didn't go to boarding school and I didn't have these experiences that it seemed were the requirements to enter the outdoors. I think a lot has changed since then, but it seemed to be this masculine space that I didn't see myself drawn to.

'But in Alaska, it was totally the opposite. Even though it is way more extreme, it's just life. People just live in the wilderness there, even if they are in a community. Everyone helps each other out and they lend each other clothes, and there's no hierarchy of who can be the most wildernessy because everyone has to be wildernessy there. I learned so much and people were very generous with their knowledge, and they enjoyed someone who didn't know things as opposed to making me feel bad about it. It was a chance for them maybe to share the things they liked. I had to learn a lot, from little things like how to drive on snowy roads and how to camp, to how to ride a snowmobile – all of these things. So it was a challenge to learn a lot of things that I had never known. Anyone can learn, that's the thing, but I guess there is a gate-keeping of that knowledge that happens in certain cultures, which just wasn't the case there.

'So, on the one hand, I was learning about the outdoors for the first time in my life and feeling like it was for everyone and it could be for me, and on the other hand I was healing from this trauma that I had been through and spending all this time in nature. I wasn't doing it intentionally, but suddenly what happened to me was, *oh my gosh, I want to take pictures again.* To me, proof that I was healing was hearing my brain say, *this is a story I want to tell,* but also it was like my body was telling me, *you need to be in this place.* This place is a healing place and it's slower and in the outdoors and it's still exciting; you still have to take bush planes to get anywhere and there are still lots of people around. So it all worked out that way for me.

'Of course, it is still a really masculine place and you are still dealing with sexism in many ways, and in a place like Alaska there are just fewer women than men, but the women that are there are so tough and so cool. I was photographing the dog sled races, which is one of the only co-ed professional sports, and I would meet all these women who are my age racing sled dogs across a thousand miles of wilderness. They were so badass and they were so nice and they weren't competitive. They didn't have that macho thing; they are all friends with each other, and helpful. So it was really wonderful to join, photograph and become friends with these awesome women out there.

'There were things that I used to be so intimidated by – like wildlife photography. I photograph people and their relationship with animals, and I photograph climate change, but now I am doing wildlife photography too, which is something I never thought I could do. It is a very masculine profession and a masculine space, and a lot of it was learning from someone who did it. Those opportunities aren't given to women as frequently, mostly just because what wildlife photographers need is someone to carry stuff. They need someone really strong to carry stuff.'

I know where she is coming from with that, and so I ask her how was it going out there on her own.

'There was a time when I was never being a woman alone in the woods,' Katie says, 'because I would usually have a guide for safety, but I had lots of experiences where I felt that I might have been better doing this on my own. On this most recent shoot, I did go out on my own and I had this really amazing experience happen where a wolf came right up to me. I don't think that would have happened if I had been with somebody else. I think part of it was exactly because I was alone. I read recently that that will happen more frequently with women, that they will approach you, and so I think being in this space, and being relaxed, is something that is really important for getting those magical encounters where animals are curious about you as opposed to you sneaking up on them.

'I've been doing this story now with caribou for about two years and how they are in decline. Caribou are one of the most important animals for people in the north but they are also a crucial part of the entire ecosystem in the Arctic. Their decline is telling us that there are problems with the whole system, and photographing them has been really special. The females are the leaders – the male caribou just follow them – and so when I was photographing the migration it was just me and all the lady caribou, which was a really nice moment. All these animals around me were female, and here I was by myself with them and I felt good and I felt safe. And that definitely isn't the way I might have felt a decade ago.

'It's been really healing but also I've learned so much. I want to keep encouraging women to do this kind of work because it traditionally relates to hunting and fishing and learning things from your father, and that's really not the case for so many female photographers, but there is space for them in this field. And, in fact, what they think might be drawbacks are advantages. Instead of thinking, *I don't know how to hunt and fish and all these things*, just being out there and really loving the animals and being low-key and taking landscape photos is OK, and they might approach you because you have that calm energy and they are curious about you, especially if you are alone.

'I understand being a bit fearful of being alone in the woods, especially as a woman, but it's been a really awesome experience for me. I'm always on my own when I'm working. Sometimes I team up with a writer, but generally I'm travelling on my own and going out and working with a subject. Camping by myself was something I only started doing for the caribou story and the healing wilderness story. Women have a tendency to want to please, so whoever we are with – even if you are the boss per se – you are worried about the other person, so it's really freeing to be alone because you aren't trying to please anybody, and if there is a mistake it's yours. That has been really special.

'When you are in indigenous communities, people find you. I have been photographing subsistence hunting and the most I have learned about caribou has come from people in indigenous communities, like this one community Anaktuvuc Pass in Alaska. It's a Nunamiut community, which means "people of the land", and they've been hunting and living with and depending on these caribou for millennia. When you go there it's always a woman who adopts you if you are an outsider and you are just visiting. Some elder or some woman will just become your friend and then that is how you start to learn about things. They might not be the hunters who you go out with, but when you come back they know just as much about the animal and they will be processing and cooking the meat, and sometimes they do go out and hunt. I enter these communities and begin learning because of this female space – which people don't really think of because they think I'm just going to go out with the hunters – but it is the whole process of bringing the meat to the house, butchering it, making the food and bringing everyone together. It's been really nice to spend time with women and learn all about that with them and their connection with the animals, and then to go out there and have my own experience with the animals.'

'So are you destined to spend your life in the wilderness now?' I ask, knowing that Katie still lives in the city, and it makes her laugh.

'Back here in NYC, gardening is my big hobby and I love plants. I try to bring as much nature into my living space as possible,' she replies, echoing the words of all the women I have spoken to, each saying that you can always do something.

'We feel this affinity for nature,' I say. 'What do you think it is?'

'I mean it's got to be biological, it has to be in us. When I was a kid I loved nature in certain ways, but it's a shame the way we teach people about the outdoors – it was always associated with strenuous physical activity. Growing up, it meant that you were going on a hike or going cross-country skiing, which I hated, or doing something that was unpleasant. I don't blame my parents, because they hadn't discovered how healing it could be for themselves, so I would learn about it in school or in camp or in some way that made it associated with negative things. So getting people into the outdoors in a way that isn't so masculine or competitive or based on sports or farming or gardening is wonderful. Maybe that isn't for everybody, but there is something in nature that *does* speak to everyone and so it is important to nurture that in young people so they find out what that is.

'I was thirty when I came to it,' she laughs. 'I spent my whole life thinking I was just this city person, that I didn't like this stuff, but what I didn't like was the capitalism and masculinity of it all – until I went to this wild place like Alaska where there were lots of indigenous people who have held on to this relationship with nature that has been lost in modern society. The people who choose to live there are really aware of how important nature and the wild is for people. I discovered it there, but you shouldn't have to go that far! I could have just gone to upstate New York, but I had it stuck in my head that nature wasn't a place for me, that it was a place for other people. Finding out that nature is a place for everyone was really special.'

I have this image of a vast landscape with a tiny tent and a tiny Katie in the middle of it, and I ask her what her favourite memories are.

'What was really neat was this wolf experience. My big fear about camping alone for the caribou story was predators because caribou are this ultimate prey, so I was very scared about bears. I'm not going to bring a gun because I'm not going to use it; if I ever needed a gun, that would be that, because I'm not going to be good enough at it. I had everything else: I had bear spray, a bear fence for my tent, I had an air-horn, a flare gun – all these things so that I'm not going to get eaten by a bear or have a scary bear encounter. I have had a few and they have always been when I've been with men who are overconfident or forgot their bear spray and I would be relying on someone else's knowledge. So this time I was completely prepared.

'The scariest thing is a bear with a cub because they are so protective. So the worst thing you can do is just accidentally stumble across a bear and cub and accidentally get in between the two of them, but that can just happen if you are going through a pass or a bunch of rocks or something. I had been photographing the caribou and I see what looked to me in the far distance like a mum and baby bear running, and I'm thinking, *oh man! No!* It's light all day long in Alaska, right? So I barely slept because it was so light and there were caribou everywhere and I was pretty manic and just taking little naps. I thought, *oh shoot, I'm overtired*, but I was ready and waiting for this bear. I look a little closer and I realise it's loping and I'm like, *why are these bears loping?* Then I realised it was a big wolf with a white stripe down the middle of it so from afar it looked like two separate animals. Then I realised I didn't know what to do. Why is it running towards me? Wolves don't approach people, especially in the Arctic; they don't want anything to do with people, so I couldn't work out what was happening and it was still running towards me. I know there haven't really been any wolf attacks that wasn't an odd situation with an odd animal since the late 1970s or something. I know all this, but I'm by myself so I'm focusing on checking if I am near a den. I got so scared and part of that was because I was alone and, although I had been so ready for bears, I wasn't ready for wolves.

'It runs up to me, to a short distance away, and then it just starts rubbing its belly on a rock and rolling around and looking really goofy. I was thinking, *is that a dog?* Because it was acting so goofy. It ended up sticking around and I took some bad photos of it because I realised it wasn't a danger, and after a while it ran off. No one was there but I guess it felt I wasn't scary, I wasn't threatening. And I was only scared at first because I was alone and tired, but when it went off I really wanted it to come back. When I spoke to elders in the community afterwards, they said it must have been an adolescent who had never seen a person before and it was just thinking, *what is this?* It was just the coolest experience.

'In this caribou story, we have also been photographing lots of the solutions to the problems for the caribou and the local indigenous people created by climate change. It's mostly indigenous communities that are doing these really exciting efforts to either grow herds that were on the edge of extinction or keep herds from getting there. One of those First Nations communities is the West Moberly First Nations and the other is the Saulteau, in British Colombia, so this was the Klinse-Za caribou herd, which was at the edge of extinction. It was at seven animals and now is at a hundred. They have been running this maternity programme where they capture pregnant females and then during the most vulnerable time of the year – giving birth and caring for the calves for the first two months – they keep them in a pen, where they are protected from predators and they can supplement their food and get them strong and healthy for when they release them back into the wild.

'I was with biologists that are part of the programme and this helicopter pilot, and we were there to see if there were any caribou out there to capture. We didn't find any but there was a collar out there, sending out data from a caribou that had been eaten, so they wanted to go and retrieve that collar. We landed and went out – and it was spring, when bears are coming out of hibernation – and then we got chased by a grizzly and it was terrifying. I'm with the helicopter pilot high up, and the biologists further down the hill start yelling, "The bear is coming!" I'm shouting, "Hey bear!" to ward it off, and the helicopter pilot is too cool to even do the things where you start yelling and making noise at the bears. I'm the only one making the noise and huffing and puffing up the hill.'

We are both laughing as Katie tells me this, both knowing that fear and the inability to run through snow.

'It was so scary,' she says, 'and it came really close and false-charged us and then swerved off and went in the other direction.

'Humility is really important, the ability to be very upfront about what you do and don't know. I still know so little about the outdoors and wild animals and how to work there, and I think there is an advantage in being a woman because you are not afraid of asking questions and admitting how much you don't know and how much help you might need. That is so important because everywhere is different and in each area local knowledge is so specific.'

'Well, after covering this story you probably know an awful lot more than most people about caribou now. Tell me more about them,' I say.

'The caribou lifestyle is all about the birth cycle. It's all about the survival of the species. Arctic caribou will go hundreds – sometimes thousands – of miles between their feeding, breeding and wintering grounds. There are two things that the migration has to do with: birth and mosquitoes. They will travel to their birthing grounds like clockwork. They can be hundreds of miles apart and they will all know when it's time and they will just meet each other and begin this journey. They have a magnetic north

– they are just this incredible animal – and they all head to these breeding grounds.

'They have their babies and then continue the migration north to escape the mosquitoes and get to a high windy area where the calves can feed. From there, they'll go back to their wintering grounds and the cycle starts all over.

'One of the major issues with the collapse of these populations occurs when there is development along this migration trail, especially in the birthing grounds. These are places where they have been going for thousands of years, and there are specific lichen that's really good and nutritious for their calves. There is safety in numbers for the caribou, so they move in these huge herds to scare away predators. They almost move like an insect swarm and having a big group is always safe for them; they have learned that they need a lot of space and a lot of animals to survive. Once a population reduces to a certain level it gets critical. They need to be in the hundreds or thousands.

'The Porcupine caribou herd – the only one that isn't decreasing right now but actually growing – is located in the Arctic wildlife refuge, which the Gwich'in people and other activists have been successful in protecting from drilling up until now. They have kept the area free of development so the caribou can get to that breeding area and continue their migration.

'The folks that have been living in harmony with these animals for so many years have specific traditions, like they don't hunt the first caribou that pass through their village because the strong healthy females always lead the migration, so they will wait to get the males or the middle of the herd. Essentially, they have done a traditional version of species management just in the way they are hunting. These are things that don't get listened to by state management and are one of the reasons why we are seeing this collapse. In Canada they are starting to incorporate indigenous knowledge in species management and the science that they are doing about caribou, but it's a little late. We are hoping that the US can learn from Canada's mistakes and not let these herds go extinct.

'The males don't really seem to do much. They amble along and show up, sometimes they can be protective if they are in a group, and they might come and check us humans out, but generally their time to shine is their rut. In the fall they start losing their coat, and then the males especially get big beautiful antlers – in caribou both the males and females have antlers but the males get really big – and their coat gets beautiful and gorgeous and then there is the rut. They are trying to attract mates, so they fight with each other and they mate. That's pretty much all they do other than follow the ladies around for the rest of the year.

'In terms of the humans that live there . . . I'm not going to idealise, there are still issues like sexism in communities, but there is so much deep respect for elders and that goes beyond gender. In the communities that have been keeping the Arctic wildlife refuge safe, some of the main activists there have been women. Oftentimes it is elders, and they are hugely important in terms of their knowledge and their stories. There are more women that are elders, and that knowledge is so precious and they mean everything to the communities there. There is this hugely important element of this natural world and all the cycles of life. It's a symbiotic relationship as opposed to an extractive relationship that seems so much more masculine – industry and war and colonisation and all that. I think the conservation world needs to learn a lot from indigenous people.

'I'm thinking particularly of this idea, often in the roots of conservation, that we need to preserve an area so that we can use it for recreation. Who was really using land for recreation a hundred years ago? Men.

'So, people like Aldo Leopold who have done so much for conservation and protecting the American wilderness, recognising that they are still coming from this place where

they are claiming that a landscape is pristine. As if people
haven't been living there and using it for thousands of years,
because they have. Then colonising it and wanting to
protect it for men to pursue the things that make them feel
closer to nature, as opposed to women. That is even reflected
in the rules; for example, you aren't allowed to gather or
collect herbs from the environment, which might be more
of a female or indigenous pursuit, but you can go on a
rafting trip. We need to rethink where those rules we have
for wilderness have come from and why they are the way
they are.'

Aldo Leopold is famous amongst ecologists as someone
who first started to write about some really significant
ecological ideas in his book, *A Sand Country Almanac*,
which is a beautiful read for anyone interested in the natural
world.[1] Despite the book being published back in 1949,
those ideas still hold enormous validity today. Significantly,
he described, before wolves were even reintroduced back
into Yellowstone, how the impact of their absence affected
the rest of the ecosystem – the idea of the 'trophic cascade'.

Leopold also wrote about man being 'only a member of a
biotic team', an idea that we are part of an ecological system
of natural balances and checks which he repeatedly describes.
And his book echoes with the call of *Homo sapiens*' lost
contact with nature and its implications.

In 'Conservation Esthetic', an essay in the third,
philosophical segment of the book, Leopold illuminates the
paradox of humans appreciating the need to 'get back to
nature', yet doing so in a way that is self-defeating. 'Like ions
shot from the sun,' he writes, 'the weekenders radiate from
every town, generating heat and friction as they go' until,
'antlike, he (man) swarms the continents' and as a
consequence Leopold bemoans the fact that there is really
very little untouched wilderness or real solitude left.

As Katie mentions, Leopold describes the relationship
between man and recreation; hunting, fishing and the like as

a poor substitute for that contact with nature which, previously, humans had to have simply in order to survive. However, so far, it has been recreation for which most wilderness has been protected.

I think Katie is right to bring it up – a man ahead of his time, querying our approach, our separation from the natural world, and our modern, miserable attempts to reconnect. To identify that he talks about the man–land relationship.

Leopold even debates the idea that, 'In human history, we have learned (I hope) that the conqueror role is eventually self-defeating. Why? Because it is implicit in such a role that the conqueror knows, *ex cathedra*, just what makes the community clock tick, and just what and who is valuable, and what and who is worthless, in community life. It always turns out that he knows neither, and this is why his conquests eventually defeat themselves.'

I find it also notable that only one woman is mentioned in the whole book, Margaret Morse Nice, an amateur ornithologist who published much groundbreaking research on birds. Other than that, the book focuses on the relationship between man and nature in every way, repeatedly discussing the man–earth drama for example. For a man so ahead of his time, I guess in one way perhaps he wasn't.

So how do we rethink the rules, in the way Katie describes? Perhaps we start, as she is, by acknowledging those communities who have had a different relationship with the land for many centuries and re-examining our man–earth drama and rules, this time with some respect.

———

'These communities in the Arctic,' Katie continues, 'would still be nomadic and follow the caribou and seasons if they could, but it was mandated in the 1950s that these communities had to choose a village site and they were forced to live in one place. Now, no one is truly nomadic in the Arctic in that sense. It is illegal for your kids not to go to school, so they have to be there. There are these rules in place that make certain things difficult, but they have subsistence leave and there is a certain amount of time that a family can take the kids out of school because they are going to go out on the land and learn. That is so important and something that would be great for any kid. I think about how I thought I didn't like science growing up because I thought it was just memorising things – I didn't realise being a biologist could mean being outside and doing all this fun stuff.

'Especially in this time of climate change, communities that might have been more gendered are opening up skills more like hunting. There are more women hunting now because they just want people to know these skills and pass them on. I'll go out with women to gather herbs for tea, get blueberries, gather eggs, fishing . . . Women less often will be using rifles to hunt animals but they will still be out on the land, gathering and doing subsistence and getting food.

'The elders there will have seen every caribou migration for almost the last century, and that's not data that anybody at the government wildlife services or any university has. They really have the key to the knowledge that we need for conservation and fighting the climate crisis, and they are ageing and we are losing them so it is so important – in a way that the villages and communities feel comfortable – for them to store and share that knowledge and also for people to listen to it and incorporate it and not see it as folklore because it is scientific.'

'One more thing,' I ask, and Katie smiles at my tone, but then she's always smiling. 'Have you ever hugged a tree?'

'Yes!'

'And?'

'It's great! The more I think about the past, I think I have actually been so drawn to nature. I've done things like that since I was a kid. I would find these special places and hug trees and it always just makes you feel good. As simple as taking a walk in the park makes you feel good, spending time in these places makes me feel good. I was thinking this is where I want to do my work so that I can be in these places that make me feel good. I spend so much time working that I wanted to make sure that time was in nature at least. It's very healing. Growing up so much in New York City, everything is larger than life, then you go out into nature and you realise, *oh I'm nothing, I'm so small and insignificant.* You go to these big cities and everybody feels like they are so important and that they are in the centre of the world or something and it makes you feel so big. It's the opposite in nature, it makes you feel tiny and that's a beautiful feeling, like you have no control and you are insignificant but you are part of something that's really big.'

Hugging the Bloody Tree

I'm actually quite irritated about it, but I need to hug a tree and find out what it really feels like. That irritation has resulted in me putting it off and putting it off as I have written this book, even though I've researched tree-hugging, even though I've learned about the science and benefits of being close to trees and hugging trees, and even though I've spoken to and read about amazing wild women, for whom I have the upmost admiration, who have openly confessed to hugging trees. So now I find myself on the final stretch of my trail to find the wild woman, having not actually hugged a tree because, for some reason unknown to me, I have been stubbornly resistant to it.

Now appears to be the time to do it.

I casually amble out into the garden and across the bridge and realise I am actually looking around furtively. I'm embarrassed despite there being no one to see me (because I have, of course, waited for everyone to go out).

Which tree? I've planted so many trees in the time that I've lived here: silver birch, oak, cherry, willows, many fruit trees and that little ornamental maple tree that my mum gave me, which is particularly beautiful. For lightness of spirit, maybe I should try the silver birch? Or perhaps the solid character of the oak? I look around with new eyes.

The old beech tree is so big that it might have even been here when the first mill-house was built. Perhaps it even pre-dates the weir it overlooks. It certainly watched the evolution from donkey paddock to vegetable patch and all the trials and tribulations that went with me trying to grow vegetables. Just across the river from the house, it has watched our comings and goings ever since we got here more than twenty years ago. It has seen the children grow from babies to men, observed the chaos of our kitchen and every breakfast, supper, drunken dinner party, cake baking disaster and midnight snack. It has seen puppies grow into old dogs and has two of them buried underneath it, it has watched a baby otter rescued and released as an adult and seen us cross the bridge together and apart, laughing and in tears. This huge tree has borne witness to so many of the dramas of my tiny life.

And I have watched the beech too – through every season, through its glorious gold to its fresh lime spring, from the sun rising behind it to the evenings when its front is caste with an orange glow. It has been my first view every morning from the bedroom as it bends in a storm or reliably bursts once more with new life, always there. I love all the trees but I *really* love this tree. I probably know it best since I see it the most, so I guess that if there is anything at all in this idea, the history of this tree means it might be the most understanding. So, the beech it is.

I cross the stream. The water is low and clear, ferns droop, and green reed spears are just beginning to come through on its banks. The sun is low but the birds are singing loudly. Snowdrops have made their appearance official this weekend and I feel relief to see them around the bottom of the tree alongside thrusting daffodil leaves; a long gloomy winter will soon be over. The golden leaves of last summer crunch at my feet.

I wonder if the tree already knows what I'm about to do; some say it can feel my vibrations. Perhaps it's laughing its head off. No, wait, it's a tree.

So here goes . . . no need to overthink it, a step forward, arms wide and I'm hugging the tree.

The bark is smooth and cold on my cheek. I push my hands all the way round, and I still don't even think I'm halfway. I get my feet, belly and chest right up to it; a proper hug, and I wait for something to happen.

An insect falls down into my jumper. I don't release my grip on the tree.

At least this is better than bramble-bashing, I think, remembering the weeping and wailing machete woman.

Above me, birds chant, branches arch.

This tree is so big up close. It's comforting to hug something so solid, so much bigger than me, so . . . always there. I miss that.

Involuntarily, I take a huge breath and let it out . . . I'm fine. I'm actually breathing slower, I didn't realise I needed to.

The river washes below us. The sky is turning pink. I notice buds on the tips of the branches – another whisper of spring, of hope.

I'm calm. Nothing dramatic happens – no whooshing exchange of energy for me and the beech – but something low in my chest lets go. I feel fine, actually deeply fine.

It's getting cold, and quite funny really.

What a marvellous thing – to be able to hug a tree you have known so well for almost a quarter of a century. Joyous, in fact.

Ah! Joy, hello, there you are. It bubbles in my belly, reaching my lips and turning the corners upward as I try not to laugh at myself and to take this seriously.

Now, how long does one hug a tree? And what is the done thing here? I mean afterwards, does one quietly exit or make another date with a view to future dates, or suggest that we simply remain casual acquaintances and observers of each other's lives as we have been until this moment.

I step back, releasing my grip and find myself mumbling, 'Thank you, that was lovely, we'll probably do it again. I'll come back.'

I head over the bridge to the house.

What exactly happened there? Whatever it was, it's enough to make me think I actually might try it more often. But only when no one is looking because, even if it does feel nice, the last label any wild woman wannabe like me needs is 'tree-hugger'.

Kettle on in the kitchen, my gaze, as it does on countless moments every day, automatically falls on the beech tree through the window. It hasn't changed one bit in response to our embrace.

But where am I at? Where did this trail lead me?

Yes, there is now joy. Yes, there is still love. And yes, there is also a deep sadness. But somewhere between the chainsawing, swimming, growing, striving, creature watching, plant observing and the stories of so many other wild women, the depression that was so stuck has shifted. I remember my simple place in nature's world, that it is bigger than the cycles of my life or the agonies of my heart, that it means more to my health than even I had realised, and, that, whether its power comes from a place of science, evolution or mysticism, ultimately all that really matters is that it makes me *me* again; just a human being.

Notes

Chapter Two: What Really is a Wild Woman, then?

1. Campbell, J. 1988. *Joseph Campbell and the Power of Myth, 'Love and the Goddess'*. TV Interview with Bill Moyers.
2. Ibid.
3. Pinkola Estés, C. 2008. *Women Who Run with the Wolves: Contacting the Power of the Wild Woman*. Rider, London.
4. Ibid., p. 3.
5. Ibid., p. 4.

Chapter Three: Memories – Scrambled Brain Anyone?

1. Green, L. G. 1976. *Karoo*. Timmins, Cape Town.

Chapter Nine: Woodswoman

1. LaBastille, A. 1991. *Woodswoman*. Penguin, London.

Chapter Ten: It isn't Just Tree Hugging

1. Wilson, E. O. 1984. *Biophilia*. Harvard University Press, Cambridge, MA.
2. Furuyashiki, A., Tabuchi, K., Norikoshi, K., Kobayashi, T. & Oriyama, S. 2019. A comparative study of the physiological and psychological effects of forest bathing (Shinrin-yoku) on working age people with and without depressive tendencies. *Environmental Health and Preventative Medicine* 24(1): 46.
3. Antonelli, M., Donelli, D., Barbieri, G., Valussi, M., Maggini, V. & Firenzuoli, F. 2020. Forest Volatile Organic Compounds and Their Effects on Human Health: A State-of-the-Art Review. *International Journal of Environmental Research and Public Health* 17(18): 6506.
4. Bratman, G. N., Hamilton, J. P., Hahn, K. S., Daily, G. C. & Gross, J. J. 2015. Nature experience reduces rumination and subgenus prefrontal cortex activation. *Proceedings of the National Academy of Sciences* 112 (28): 8567–8572.
5. Ulrich, R. S. 1984. View through a window may influence recovery from surgery. *Science* 224(4647): 420–421.
6. Lowry C. A. *et al.* 2007. Identification of an immune-responsive mesolimbocortical serotonergic system: Potential role in regulation of emotional behavior. *Neuroscience* 146(2): 756–772.
7. Louv, R. 2010. *Last Child in the Woods: Saving Our Children from Nature-Deficit Disorder*. Atlantic Books, London.

Chapter Thirteen: Looking Back Again

1. Johanson, D. & Edey, M. 1981. *Lucy: The Beginnings of Humankind*. Warner Books, NY.
2. Lovejoy, C. O. 1981. The Origin of Man. *Science* 211: 4480.

Chapter Fourteen: A Rewrite?

1. Krems, J. A., Claessens, S., Fales, M. R., Campenni, M., Haselton, M. G. & Aktipis, A. 2021. An agent-based model of the female rivalry hypothesis for concealed ovulation in humans. *Nature Human Behaviour* 5: 726–735.
2. Ibid.
3. Ibid.
4. Cirotteau, T., Kerner, J., Pincas, E. & Hurd, P. 2022. *Lady Sapiens: Breaking Stereotypyes About Prehistoric Women.* Hero, London.
5. Universitaet Tübingen. 2014. Humans and saber-toothed tiger met in Germany 300,000 years ago. *ScienceDaily.*

Chapter Fifteen: A Fascination for Plants

Ridley, G. 2011. *The Discovery of Jeanne Baret: A Story of Science, the High Seas, and the First Woman to Circumnavigate the Globe.* Crown, London.

Chapter Eighteen: When Doing What it Takes Doesn't Work

1. Investigation Team Report. 2010. *Attacks by a grizzly bear in Soda Butte Campground on the Gallatin National Forest on July 28, 2010.*
2. Yellowstone Insider, 2020. *Attacking Soda Butte bear was sick, stressed; she snapped.*

Chapter Twenty-seven: The Killer Menopause

1. Lauren, J., Brent, N., Franks, D. W., Foster, E. A., Balcomb, K. C., Cant, M. A., & Croft, D. P. 2015. Ecological Knowledge, Leadership, and the Evolution of Menopause in Killer Whales. *Current Biology* 25:6.
2. Whitehead, H. 2015. Life History Evolution: What does a menopausal killer whale do? *Current Biology* 25:6.
3. Hawkes, K., O'Connell, J. F., Blurton Jones, N. G., Alvarez, H. & Charnov, E. L. 1998. Grandmothering, menopause, and the evolution of human life histories. *Anthropology* 95: 1336–1339.
4. Ibid.

Chapter Twenty-eight: A State of Awe

1. Leopold, A. 2020. *A Sand Country Almanac: And Sketches Here and There.* Penguin, London.

Acknowledgements

I hope the stories of our connection with the natural world in this book are inspiring, that they arouse even more curiosity about the qualities we all have and that, above all, they empower us to look again at the extraordinary wealth and value of the natural world around us. I owe a massive thanks to each woman who took the time, care and (sometimes) vulnerability in sharing her story. Each had the power to make me both laugh and cry, sometimes at the same time as they shared their wisdom.

My thanks to Sarah Tompkins at Samara, Nyaradzu Hoto and Damien Mander at Akashinga, Liza Gadsby at Pandrillus Foundation, Athena Aktipis at Arizona State University, Jan Gaertner, Doris Florig, Pippa Ehrlich, Angela Scott and Katie Orlinsky. They represent a long tradition of millions of amazing women out there, doing this stuff quietly for generations to come.

Of course, this is a book about women, but I also want to thank the many men who have taught me about the power of the natural world through my life, from lecturers and writers to adventurers, wildlife rescuers, film makers and vets.

My agent Gill McLay deserves all the thanks in the world and so much love for her generous supply of fish and chips and book talk, for endless convoluted discussions and for crafting and cajoling me into the semblance of a writer and of course to the ever supportive John McLay who knows how to wield an Emma Bridgewater mug.

Julie, my editor at Bloomsbury, whose patience and understanding have been incomparable as I wove my way through the discovery of what this book would be and then battled with the demons to write it. Thank you in so many ways, I promise I will never make you wait that long again.

Jenny Campbell at Bloomsbury, thank you so much for all your hard work and support.

The marketing team at Bloomsbury, especially Sarah Head and the publicity team, especially Jess Gray have worked so hard and I really appreciate it. It takes a special team to work with the care that you do. Thanks also go to Jasmine Parker for designing such a beautiful cover.

There are so many women in my life to thank for their endless support and love, especially through some bonkers times: Hilary Knight, Tina Price, Julie Elledge, Kaitlin Yarnell, you have kept my north star clear.

My thanks to my mum as ever who has shown me what a strong woman is and the simple power of a garden and a love for nature.

And every woman who buoys up another and knows the power of a walk in the woods, a cycle under the mountains, a dip in a lake, an amble around the garden and a conversation. Each of my friends you know who you are and how priceless.

And of course to my sons, Fred, Gus and Arthur, who bring meaning, love and laughter to every day and are all just fantastic! And of course I will thank Doodle too! ... and Zen the cat in my inbox . . . every writer needs a dog by their feet and a cat in their inbox to stay even a little sane.

Index